The History of the Reign of King Henry VII

Francis Bacon

ET REMOTISSIMA PROPE

.

Published by Hesperus Press Limited
4 Rickett Street, London sw6 1ru
www.hesperuspress.com

First published in 1622
First published by Hesperus Press Limited, 2007

Foreword © Brian Thompson, 2007

Designed and typeset by Fraser Muggeridge studio
Printed in Jordan by the Jordan National Press

ISBN: 1-84391-708-4
ISBN13: 978-1-84391-708-3

CONTENTS

In 1605, King James I visited the Bodleian Library, the brainchild and preoccupation of the former Elizabethan diplomat and courtier, Sir Thomas Bodley. In a wonderfully dry phrase, explaining how he had cast about for a new way of serving the state that lay comfortably 'out of the throng of court contentions', Sir Thomas told how he resolved 'to set up my staff at the library door in Oxon'. Though he was offered inducements to return to political office under the new monarch, he found them easy to resist. Bodley had found something to do with his talents that brought him greater joy and contentment than the old round of court intrigue.

One of the people who wrote to him in that year was the lawyer and courtier Francis Bacon. Bacon's greatest political achievements were still to come and he made this curious admission to Bodley: 'I do confess, since I was of any understanding, my mind has in effect been absent from what I have done.' And to drive the point home: 'I have led my life in civic causes, for which I was not very fit by nature, and more unfit by the preoccupation of my mind.'

This reads like classic Baconian guile. Was he offering Bodley an elegantly couched compliment, all the better for being so oblique, or were his remarks a real and rueful confession? It was the year the scholarly lawyer published *The Advancement of Learning*, but that only muddies the waters further. Who knew what this letter actually meant?

Because, for someone as unfit for purpose as he claimed to be, Bacon's star was rising. Two years after this letter, he was appointed Solicitor General. In 1613 (the year of Bodley's death) he was Attorney General. Four years after that, Sir Francis Bacon became Lord Keeper of the Great Seal and Lord Chancellor and was elevated to the peerage as Lord Verulam. There was no cleverer – nor more nimble-minded – man in the Jacobean court.

Then, in 1621, the axe fell. Bacon was stripped of all his offices, fined an unpayably huge sum of money, sent to the Tower (briefly) and ordered to quit London. He retreated to his house at Gorhambury outside St Albans, as comprehensively unpersonned as any Soviet apparatchik in the days of Stalin. And only now does the letter he wrote to Bodley in 1605 begin to make sense.

In fourteen weeks, from June to October, using only the materials available in his own library, Bacon wrote *The History of the Reign of King Henry VII*, considered to be the first modern classic of English history and, additionally, a genuine work of literature. Such double accolades do not happen by accident: Bacon poured into this book the distillation of a lifetime's reading and an insider's experience of how high politics actually works.

For the modern reader, one of the guilty pleasures the book provides is to remind one of half-remembered stories first heard in drowsy schoolrooms. The two pretty-boy Yorkist impostors, Lambert Simnel and Perkin Warbeck ('this little cockatrice') and a third, Ralph Wilford, are dealt with by a savage briskness not often found in history teachers. The story of how Warbeck dragged the hapless young Earl of Warwick, his fellow prisoner in the Tower, into a plot to usurp Henry VII reads like a Hollywood treatment.

So, too, Bacon's account of the bewildered Cornishmen who were persuaded to take on the crown in a dispute about taxation with nothing more than bow and arrows. They advanced on London and were boxed up on Blackheath by the King's army: 2,000 of them were slaughtered.

Bacon asks an interesting question about this event. If the 'Kentish commotion' of 1495 (engineered by the unlovable Warbeck) had been put down with over 150 executions, how was it that only three leaders paid the price among the Cornishmen? His answer is characteristically elegant: the King wished to distinguish between wantonness and want.

And this, it seems to me, brings us to the real heart of the text – the portrait of Henry VII himself. Bacon leaves us with the feeling that there was more to Henry than is told here, not for want of evidence, or the author's ignorance of human motive, but as the inevitable pre-condition of historical writing. His King is not unlike Bacon himself, high-minded, yet frustrated by circumstance. He does great things during his reign, as befits the Tudor myth. But his biographer imbues him with some of the frailties he himself possessed. Chief among these is what amounts to spiritual anxiety. In the repeated attempts to explain and justify himself, a man's certainties begin to totter. He ends up not knowing exactly who he is.

Bacon's genius is to show that, even among absolute monarchs, will is not everything. In the old chronicles, a king did what he did because he had the power to do it. What is new in this work is its psychological depth. With Bacon's help, we can 'explain' Henry VII's reign and trace some of his actions to their origins – an exile's inability to nuance the country he is brought to govern, a too complaisant marriage, tight pockets when it came to rewarding loyalty. But at heart, like his biographer, we get the feeling that Henry could sense an echoing emptiness at his back. As Bacon said, of the attempt by others to understand him, 'he stood in the dark'.

– Brian Thompson, 2007

The History of the Reign of King Henry VII

It may please your Highness,

In part of my acknowledgement to your Highness, I have endeavoured to do honour to the memory of the last King of England that was ancestor to the King your father and yourself; and was that king to whom both unions may in a sort refer: that of the roses being in him consummate, and that of the kingdoms by him begun. Besides, his times deserve it. For he was a wise man, and an excellent king; and yet the times were rough, and full of mutations and rare accidents. And it is with times as it is with ways. Some are more uphill and downhill, and some are more flat and plain; and the one is better for the liver, and the other for the writer. I have not flattered him, but took him to life as well as I could, sitting so far off, and having no better light. It is true, your Highness has a living pattern, incomparable, of the King your father. But it is not amiss for you also to see one of these ancient pieces. God preserve your Highness.

Your Highness' most humble
and devoted servant,

Francis St Alban

After that Richard, the third of that name, king in fact only, but tyrant both in title and regiment, and so commonly termed and reputed in all times since, was by the Divine Revenge, favouring the design of an exiled man, overthrown and slain at Bosworth Field,[1] there succeeded in the kingdom the Earl of Richmond, thenceforth styled Henry the Seventh.[2] The King immediately after the victory, as one that had been bred under a devout mother and was in his nature a great observer of religious forms, caused *Te Deum Laudamus* to be solemnly sung in the presence of the whole army upon the place, and was himself with general applause and great cries of joy, in a kind of military election or recognition, saluted King.

Meanwhile the body of Richard after many indignities and reproaches (the *dirigies* and obsequies of the common people towards tyrants) was obscurely buried. For though the King of his nobleness gave charge unto the friars of Leicester to see an honourable interment to be given to it, yet the religious people themselves (being not free from the humours of the vulgar) neglected it, wherein nevertheless they did not then incur any man's blame or censure. No man thinking any ignominy or contumely worthy of him, that had been the executioner of King Henry the Sixth (that innocent prince)[3] with his own hands; the contriver of the death of the Duke of Clarence, his brother;[4] the murderer of his two nephews (one of them his lawful King in the present, and the other in the future, failing of him);[5] and vehemently suspected to have been the empoisoner of his wife, thereby to make vacant his bed for a marriage within the degrees forbidden.[6] And although he were a prince in military virtue approved, jealous of the honour of the English nation, and likewise a good lawmaker for the ease and solace of the common people, yet his cruelties and parricides in the opinion of all men weighed down his virtues and merits; and in the opinion of wise men, even those virtues themselves were conceived to be rather feigned and affected things to serve his ambition, than true qualities ingenerate in his judgement or nature.

And therefore it was noted by men of great understanding (who seeing his after-acts looked back upon his former proceedings) that even in the time of King Edward his brother he was not without secret trains and mines to turn envy and hatred upon his brother's government, as having an expectation and a kind of divination that the King, by reason of his many disorders, could not be of long life, but was like to leave his sons of tender years; and then he knew well how easy a step it was from the place of a protector and first prince of the blood to the crown. And that out of this deep root of ambition it sprang, that as well at the treaty of peace that passed between Edward the Fourth and Lewis the Eleventh of France, concluded by interview of both kings at Piqueny,[7] as upon all other occasions, Richard, then Duke of Gloucester, stood ever upon the side of honour, raising his own reputation to the disadvantage of the King his brother, and drawing the eyes of all (especially of the nobles and soldiers) upon himself; as if the King by his voluptuous life and mean marriage[8] were become effeminate, and less sensible of honour and reason of state than was fit for a king. And as for the politic and wholesome laws that were enacted in his time, they were interpreted to be but the brocage of a usurper, thereby to woo and win the hearts of the people, as being conscious to himself that the true obligations of sovereignty[9] in him failed and were wanting.

But King Henry, in the very entrance of his reign and the instant of time when the kingdom was cast into his arms, met with a point of great difficulty and knotty to solve, able to trouble and confound the wisest king in the newness of his estate; and so much the more, because it could not endure a deliberation, but must be at once deliberated and determined. There were fallen to his lot, and concurrent in his person, three several titles to the imperial crown. The first, the title of the Lady Elizabeth[10] with whom, by precedent pact with the party that brought him in, he was to marry. The second, the ancient and long disputed title (both by plea and arms)[11] of the house of Lancaster, to which he was inheritor in his own person. The third, the title of the sword or conquest for that he came in by victory of battle, and that the King in possession was slain in the field. The first of these was fairest and most like to give contentment to the people, who by two-and-twenty years' reign of King Edward the Fourth[12] had been fully made capable of the clearness of the title of the White Rose or house of York; and by the mild and plausible reign of the same king towards his latter time, were become affectionate to that line. But then it lay plain before his eyes that if he relied upon that title, he could be but a king at courtesy, and have rather a matrimonial than a regal power; the right remaining in his queen, upon whose decease, either with issue or without issue, he was to give place and be removed. And though he should obtain by parliament to be continued, yet he knew there was a very great difference between a king that holds his crown by a civil act of estates[13] and one that holds it originally by the law of nature and descent of blood. Neither wanted there even at that time secret rumours and whisperings (which afterwards gathered strength and turned to great troubles) that the two young sons[14] of King Edward the Fourth, or one of them (which were said to be destroyed in the Tower), were not indeed murdered but conveyed secretly away, and were yet living: which, if it had been true, had prevented the title of the Lady Elizabeth. On the other side, if he stood upon his own title of the house of Lancaster, inherent in his person, he knew it was a title condemned by parliament,[15] and generally prejudged in the common opinion of the realm, and that it tended directly to the disinherison of the line of York, held then the indubitable heirs of the crown. So that if he should have no issue by the Lady Elizabeth, which should be descendants of the double line, then the ancient flames of discord and intestine wars, upon the competition of both houses, would again return and revive.

As for conquest, notwithstanding Sir William Stanley, after some acclamations of the soldiers in the field, had put a crown of ornament (which Richard wore in the battle and was found amongst the spoils) upon King Henry's head, as if there were his chief title; yet he remembered well upon what conditions and agreements he was brought in, and that to claim as conqueror was to put as well his own party as the rest into terror and fear, as that which gave him power of disannulling of laws, and disposing of men's fortunes and estates, and the like points of absolute power, being in themselves so harsh and odious, as that William himself, commonly called the Conqueror,[16] howsoever he used and exercised the power of a conqueror to reward his Normans, yet he forbore to use that claim in the beginning, but mixed it with a titulary pretence, grounded upon the will and designation of Edward the Confessor.[17]

But the King, out of the greatness of his own mind, presently cast the die, and the inconveniences appearing unto him on all parts, and knowing there could not be any interreign or suspension of title, and preferring his affection to his own line and blood, and liking that title best that made him independent, and being in his nature and constitution of mind not very apprehensive or forecasting of future events afar off, but an entertainer of fortune by the day, resolved to rest upon the title of Lancaster as the main, and to use the other two, that of marriage and that of battle, but as supporters, the one to appease secret discontents, and the other to beat down open murmur and dispute; not forgetting that the same title of Lancaster had formerly maintained a possession of three descents[18] in the crown, and might have proved a perpetuity, had it not ended in the weakness and inability of the last prince. Whereupon the King presently that very day, being the two-and-twentieth of August, assumed the style of king in his own name, without mention of the Lady Elizabeth at all, or any relation thereunto. In which course he ever after persisted, which did spin him a thread of many seditions and troubles.

The King, full of these thoughts, before his departure from Leicester, despatched Sir Robert Willoughby to the castle of Sheriff-Hutton, in Yorkshire, where were kept in safe custody, by King Richard's commandment, both the Lady Elizabeth, daughter of King Edward, and Edward Plantagenet,[19] son and heir to George Duke of Clarence. This Edward was by the King's warrant delivered from the constable of the castle to the hand of Sir Robert Willoughby, and by him with all safety and diligence conveyed to the Tower of London, where he was shut up close prisoner. Which act of the King's (being an act merely of policy and power) proceeded not so much from any apprehension he had of Dr Shaw's tale[20] at Paul's Cross[21] for the bastarding of Edward the Fourth's issues, in which case this young gentleman was to succeed (for that fable was ever exploded), but upon a settled disposition to depress all eminent persons of the line of York. Wherein still the King, out of strength of will or weakness of judgement, did use to show a little more of the party[22] than of the King.

For the Lady Elizabeth, she received also a direction to repair with all convenient speed to London, and there to remain with the Queen Dowager her mother, which accordingly she soon after did, accompanied with many noblemen and ladies of honour. In the mean season the

King set forwards by easy journeys to the city of London, receiving the acclamations and applauses of the people as he went, which indeed were true and unfeigned, as might well appear in the very demonstrations and fullness of the cry. For they thought generally that he was a prince as ordained and sent down from heaven to unite and put to an end the long dissensions of the two houses, which although they had had, in the times of Henry the Fourth, Henry the Fifth, and a part of Henry the Sixth on the one side, and the times of Edward the Fourth on the other, lucid intervals and happy pauses, yet they did ever hang over the kingdom, ready to break forth into new perturbations and calamities. And as his victory gave him the knee, so his purpose of marriage with the Lady Elizabeth gave him the heart, so that both knee and heart did truly bow before him.

He on the other side with great wisdom (not ignorant of the attentions and fears of the people), to disperse the conceit and terror of a conquest, had given order that there should be nothing in his journey like unto a warlike march or manner, but rather like unto the progress of a king in full peace and assurance.

He entered the city upon a Saturday, as he had also obtained the victory upon a Saturday; which day of the week, first upon an observation, and after upon memory and fancy, he accounted and chose as a day prosperous unto him. The Mayor and companies of the city received him at Shoreditch; whence with great and honourable attendance, and troops of noblemen and persons of quality, he entered the city; himself not being on horseback, or in any open chair or throne, but in a close chariot, as one that having been sometimes an enemy to the whole state, and a proscribed person, chose rather to keep state and strike a reverence into the people than to fawn upon them. He went first into St Paul's Church, where, not meaning that the people should forget too soon that he came in by battle, he made offertory of his standards, and had orisons and *Te Deum* again sung, and went to his lodging prepared in the Bishop of London's palace, where he stayed for a time.

During his abode there, he assembled his council and other principal persons, in presence of whom he did renew again his promise to marry with the Lady Elizabeth. This he did the rather because, having at his coming out of Brittany given artificially, for serving of his own turn, some hopes, in case he obtained the kingdom, to marry Anne, inheritress to the duchy of Brittany, whom Charles the Eighth of France soon after married, it bred some doubt and suspicion amongst divers that he was not sincere, or at least not fixed, in going on with the match of England so much desired: which conceit also, though it were but talk and discourse, did much afflict the poor Lady Elizabeth herself. But howsoever he both truly intended it, and desired also it should be so believed (the better to extinguish envy and contradiction, to his other purposes), yet was he resolved in himself not to proceed to the consummation hereof, till his coronation and a parliament were past. The one, lest a joint coronation of himself and his queen might give any countenance of participation of title; the other, lest in the entailing of the crown to himself, which he hoped to obtain by parliament, the votes of the parliament might any ways reflect upon her.

About this time in autumn, towards the end of September, there began and reigned in the city and other parts of the kingdom a disease then new, which by the accidents and manner thereof they called the sweating-sickness. This disease had a swift course, both in the sick body and in the time and period of the lasting thereof. For they that were taken with it, upon four-and-twenty hours escaping were thought almost assured. And as to the time of the malice and reign of the disease ere it ceased, it began about the one-and-twentieth of September, and cleared up before the end of October; insomuch as it was no hindrance to the King's coronation, which was the last of October; nor (which was more) to the holding of the parliament, which began but seven days after. It was a pestilent fever, but as it seems not seated in the veins or humours, for that there followed no carbuncle, no purple or livid spots, or the like, the mass of the body being not tainted; only a malign vapour flew to the heart, and seized the vital spirits, which stirred nature to strive to send it forth by an extreme sweat. And it appeared by experience that this disease was rather a surprise of nature, than obstinate to remedies, if it were in time looked unto. For if the patient were kept in an equal temper, both for clothes, fire, and drink moderately warm, with temperate cordials, whereby nature's work were neither irritated by heat nor turned back by cold, he commonly recovered. But infinite persons died suddenly of it, before the manner of the cure and attendance was known. It was conceived not to be an epidemic disease, but to proceed from a malignity in the constitution of the air, gathered by the predispositions of seasons; and the speedy cessation declared as much.

On Simon and Jude's eve[23] the King dined with Thomas Bourchier, Archbishop of Canterbury, and cardinal:[24] and from Lambeth went by land over the bridge to the Tower, where the morrow after he made twelve knights-bannerets. But for creations, he dispensed them with a sparing hand. For notwithstanding a field so lately fought and a coronation so near at hand, he only created three: Jasper Earl of Pembroke (the king's uncle) was created Duke of Bedford; Thomas the Lord Stanley (the king's father-in-law) Earl of Derby; and Edward Courtney Earl of Devon; though the King had then nevertheless a purpose in himself to make more in time of parliament, bearing a wise and decent respect to distribute his creations, some to honour his coronation, and some his parliament.

The coronation followed two days after, upon the thirtieth day of October in the year of our Lord 1485. At which time Innocent the Eighth was Pope of Rome; Frederick the Third Emperor of Almain; and Maximilian his son newly chosen King of the Romans;[25] Charles the Eighth King of France; Ferdinando and Isabella Kings of Spain; and James the Third King of Scotland: with all of which kings and states the King was at that time in good peace and amity. At which day also (as if the crown upon his head had put perils into his thoughts) he did institute for the better security of his person a band of fifty archers under a captain to attend him, by the name of Yeomen-of-his-Guard: and yet that it might be thought to be rather a matter of dignity, after the imitation of that he had known abroad, than any matter of diffidence appropriate to his own case, he made it to be understood for an ordinance not temporary, but to hold in succession for ever after.

The seventh of November the King held his parliament at Westminster, which he had summoned immediately after his coming to London. His ends in calling a parliament (and that so speedily) were chiefly three. First, to procure the crown to be entailed upon himself; next to have the attainders of all his party (which were in no small number) reversed, and all acts of hostility by them done in his quarrel remitted and discharged; and on the other side, to attaint by parliament the heads and principals of his enemies. The third, to calm and quiet the fears of the rest of that party by a general pardon; not being ignorant in how great danger a king stands from his subjects, when most of his subjects are conscious in themselves that they stand in his danger. Unto these three special motives of a parliament was added, that he as a prudent and moderate prince made this judgement, that it was fit for him to hasten to let his people see that he meant to govern by law, howsoever he came in by the sword; and fit also to reclaim them to know him for their king, whom they had so lately talked of as an enemy or banished man. For that which concerned the entailing of the crown (more than that he was true to his own will, that he would not endure any mention of the Lady Elizabeth, no not in the nature of special entail), he carried it otherwise with great wisdom and measure. For he did not press to have the act penned by way of declaration or recognition of right, as on the other side he avoided to have it by new law or ordinance, but chose rather a kind of middle way, by way of establishment, and that under covert and indifferent words; 'that the inheritance of the crown should rest, remain, and abide in the king, etc.': which words might equally be applied, that the crown should continue to him; but whether as having former right to it (which was doubtful), or having it then in fact and possession (which no man denied), was left fair to interpretation either way. And again for the limitation of the entail, he did not press it to go further than to himself and to the heirs of his body, not speaking of his right heirs; but leaving that to the law to decide, so as the entail might seem rather a personal favour to him and his children, than a total disinherison to the house of York. And in this form was the law drawn and passed. Which statute he procured to be confirmed by the Pope's Bull the year following, with mention nevertheless (by way of recital) of his other titles both of descent and conquest. So as now the wreath of three was made a wreath of five. For to the three first titles, of the two houses or lines and conquest, were added two more: the authorities parliamentary and papal.

The King likewise in the reversal of the attainders of his partakers, and discharging them of all offences incident to his service and succour, had his will, and acts did pass accordingly. In the passage whereof, exception was taken to divers persons in the House of Commons, for that they were attainted, and thereby not legal, nor habilitate to serve in parliament, being disabled in the highest degree; and that it should be a great incongruity to have them to make laws who themselves were not inlawed. The truth was, that divers of those that had in the time of King Richard been strongest and most declared for the king's party,[26] were returned knights and burgesses of the parliament – whether by care or recommendation from the state, or the voluntary inclination of the people – many of which had been by Richard the Third attainted by outlawries, or otherwise. The King was somewhat troubled with this. For though it had a grave and specious show, yet it reflected upon his party. But wisely not showing himself at all moved therewith, he would not understand it but as a case in law, and wished the judges to be advised thereupon, who for that purpose were forthwith assembled in the Exchequer-chamber (which is the counsel-chamber of the judges), and upon deliberation they gave a grave and safe opinion and advice, mixed with law and convenience, which was that the knights and burgesses attainted by the course of law should forbear to come into the house till a law were passed for the reversal of their attainders. [But the judges left it there, and made no mention whether after such reversal there should need any new election or no, nor whether this sequestering of them from the house were generally upon their disability, or upon an incompetency that they should be judges and parties in their own cause. The point in law was, whether any disability in their natural capacity could trench to their politic capacity, they being but procurators of the commonwealth and representatives and fiduciaries of counties and boroughs; considering their principals stood upright and clear, and therefore were not to receive justice from their personal attainders.][27]

It was at that time incidentally moved amongst the judges in their consultation, what should be done for the King himself, who likewise was attainted. But it was with unanimous consent resolved that the crown takes away all defects and stops in blood, and that from the time the King did assume the crown the fountain was cleared, and all attainders and corruption of blood discharged. But nevertheless, for honour's sake, it was ordained by parliament that all records wherein there was any memory or mention of the King's attainder should be defaced, cancelled, and taken off the file.

But on the part of the King's enemies there were by parliament attainted, the late Duke of Gloucester, calling himself Richard the Third, the Duke of Norfolk, the Earl of Surrey, Viscount Lovel, the Lord Ferrers, the Lord Zouch, Richard Ratcliffe, William Catesby, and many others of degree and quality. In which bills of attainders, nevertheless, there were contained many just and temperate clauses, savings, and provisos, well showing and foretokening the wisdom, stay, and moderation of the King's spirit of government. And for the pardon of the rest that had stood against the King, the King upon a second advice thought it not fit it should pass by parliament, the better (being matter of grace) to impropriate the thanks to himself, using only the opportunity of a parliament time, the better to disperse it into the veins of the kingdom. Therefore during the parliament he published his royal proclamation, offering pardon and grace of restitution to all such as had taken arms or been participant of any attempts against him, so as they submitted themselves to his mercy by a day,[28] and took the oath of allegiance and fidelity to him; whereupon many came out of sanctuary, and many more came out of fear, no less guilty than those that had taken sanctuary.

As for money or treasure, the King thought it not seasonable or fit to demand any of his subjects at this parliament; both because he had received satisfaction from them in matters of so great importance, and because he could not remunerate them with any general pardon (being prevented therein by the coronation pardon passed immediately before); but chiefly, for that it was in every man's eye what great forfeitures and confiscations he had at that present to help himself; whereby those casualties of the crown might in reason spare the purses of the subject; specially in a time when he was in peace with all his neighbours. Some few laws passed at that parliament, almost for form sake: amongst which there was one to reduce aliens, being made denizens, to pay strangers' customs;[29] and another to draw to himself the seizures and compositions of Italians' goods for not employment,[30] being points of profit to his coffers, whereof from the very beginning he was not forgetful, and had been more happy at the latter end, if his early providence, which kept him from all necessity of exacting upon his people, could likewise have attempered his nature therein. He added during parliament to his former creations the ennoblement or advancement in nobility of a few others. The Lord Chandos of Brittany was made Earl of Bath; Sir Giles Daubeney was made Lord Daubeney; and Sir Robert Willoughby Lord Brooke.

The King did also with great nobleness and bounty (which virtues at that time had their turns in his nature) restore Edward Stafford, eldest son to Henry Duke of Buckingham, attainted in the time of King Richard, not only to his dignities but to his fortunes and possessions, which were great; to which he was moved also by a kind of gratitude, for that the Duke was the man that moved the first stone against the tyranny of King Richard, and indeed made the King a bridge to the crown upon his own ruins. Thus the parliament broke up.

The parliament being dissolved, the King sent forthwith money to redeem the Marquis Dorset and Sir John Bourchier, whom he had left as his pledges at Paris for money that he had borrowed when he made his expedition for England, and thereupon he took a fit occasion to send the Lord Treasurer and Mr Bray (whom he used as counsellor) to the Lord Mayor of London, requiring of the city a priest of six thousand marks.[31] But after many parleys he could obtain but two thousand pounds, which nevertheless the King took in good part, as men use to do that practise to borrow money when they have no need.

About this time the King called unto his Privy Council John Morton[32] and Richard Fox,[33] the one Bishop of Ely, the other Bishop of Exeter; vigilant men and secret, and such as kept watch with him almost upon all men else. They had been both versed in his affairs before he came to the crown, and were partakers of his adverse fortune. This Morton soon after, upon the death of Bourchier, he made Archbishop of Canterbury. And for Fox, he made him Lord Keeper of his Privy Seal, and afterwards advanced him by degrees, from Exeter to Bath and Wells, thence to Durham, and last to Winchester. For although the King loved to employ and advance bishops, because having rich bishoprics they carried their reward upon themselves, yet he did use to raise them by steps, that he might not lose the profit of the first fruits;[34] which by that course of gradation was multiplied.

At last upon the eighteenth of January was solemnised the so long expected and so much desired marriage between the King and the Lady Elizabeth; which day of marriage was celebrated with greater triumph and demonstrations (especially on the people's part) of joy and gladness than the days either of his entry or coronation, which the King rather noted than liked. And it is true that all his lifetime, while the Lady Elizabeth lived with him (for she died before him), he showed himself no very indulgent husband towards her, though she was beautiful, gentle and fruitful. But his aversion toward the house of York was so predominant in him as it found place not only in his wars and councils, but in his chamber and bed.

Towards the middle of the spring the King, full of confidence and assurance, as a prince that had been victorious in battle, and had prevailed with his parliament in all that he desired, and had the ring of acclamations fresh in his ears, thought the rest of his reign should be but play, and the enjoying of a kingdom. Yet as a wise and watchful king, he would not neglect anything for his safety, thinking nevertheless to perform all things now rather as an exercise than as a labour. So he, being truly informed that the northern parts[35] were not only affectionate to the house of York but particularly had been devoted to King Richard the Third, thought it would be a summer well spent to visit those parts, and by his presence and application of himself to reclaim and rectify those humours. But the King, in his account of peace and calms, did much over-cast his fortunes, which proved for many years together full of broken seas, tides, and tempests. For he was no sooner come to Lincoln, where he kept his Easter, but he received news that the Lord Lovel, Humphrey Stafford,[36] and Thomas Stafford, who had formerly taken sanctuary at Colchester, were departed out of sanctuary, but to what place no man could tell. Which advertisement the King despised, and continued his journey to York. At York there came fresh and more certain advertisement that the Lord Lovel was at hand with a great power of men, and that the Staffords were in arms in Worcestershire, and had made their approaches to the city of Worcester to assail it. The King, as a prince of great and profound judgement, was not much moved with it, for that he thought it was but a rag or remnant of Bosworth Field, and had nothing in it of the main party of the house of

York. But he was more doubtful of the raising of forces to resist the rebels than of the resistance itself, for that he was in a core of people whose affections he suspected. But the action enduring no delay, he did speedily levy and send against the Lord Lovel to the number of 3,000 men, ill armed but well assured (being taken some few out of his own train, and the rest out of the tenants and followers of such as were safe to be trusted), under the conduct of the Duke of Bedford. And as his manner was to send his pardons rather before the sword than after, he gave commission to the Duke to proclaim pardon to all that would come in: which the Duke, upon his approach to the Lord Lovel's camp, did perform.

And it fell out as the King expected; the heralds were the great ordnance.[37] For the Lord Lovel, upon proclamation of pardon, mistrusting his men, fled into Lancashire, and lurking for a time with Sir Thomas Broughton, after sailed over into Flanders to the Lady Margaret.[38] And his men, forsaken of their captain, did presently submit themselves to the Duke. The Staffords likewise, and their forces, hearing what had happened to the Lord Lovel (in whose success their chief trust was), despaired and dispersed, the two brothers taking sanctuary at Colnham, a village near Abingdon, which place, upon view of their privilege in the king's bench, being judged no sufficient sanctuary for traitors, Humphrey was executed at Tyburn; and Thomas, as being led by his elder brother, was pardoned. So this rebellion proved but a blast, and the King having by this journey purged a little the dregs and leaven of the northern people, that were before in no good affection towards him, returned to London.

In September following, the Queen was delivered of her first son whom the King (in honour of the British race, of which himself was) named Arthur, according to the name of that ancient worthy King of the Britons, in whose acts there is truth enough to make him famous, besides that which is fabulous. The child was strong and able, though he was born in the eighth month, which the physicians do prejudge.

There followed this year, being the second of the King's reign, a strange accident of state, whereof the relations that we have are so naked, as they leave it scarce credible; not for the nature of it (for it has fallen out), but for the manner and circumstance of it, especially in the beginnings. Therefore we shall make our judgement upon the things themselves, as they give light one to another, and (as we can) dig truth out of the mine.

The King was green in his estate, and contrary to his own opinion and desert both, was not without much hatred throughout the realm. The root of all was the discountenancing of the house of York, which the general body of the realm still affected. This did alienate the hearts of the subjects from him daily more and more, especially when they saw that after his marriage, and after a son born, the King did nevertheless not so much as proceed to the coronation of the Queen, not vouchsafing her the honour of a matrimonial crown, for the coronation of her was not till almost two years after, when danger had taught him what to do. But much more, when it was spread abroad (whether by error or the cunning malcontents) that the King had a purpose to put to death Edward Plantagenet closely in the Tower: whose case was so nearly paralleled with that of Edward the Fourth's children, in respect of the blood, like age, and the very place of the Tower, as it did refresh and reflect upon the King a most odious resemblance, as if he would be another King Richard. And all this time it was still whispered everywhere, that at least one of the children of Edward the Fourth was living. Which bruit was cunningly fomented by such as desired innovation. Neither was the King's nature and customs greatly fit to disperse these mists, but contrariwise he had a fashion rather to create doubts than assurance. Thus was fuel prepared for the spark: the spark, that afterwards kindled such a fire and combustion, was at the first contemptible.

There was a subtle priest called Richard Simons, that lived in Oxford, and had to his pupil a baker's son named Lambert Simnel,[39] of the age of some fifteen years; a comely youth, and well-favoured, not without some extraordinary dignity and grace of aspect. It came into this priest's fancy (hearing what men talked, and in hope to raise himself to some great bishopric) to cause this lad to counterfeit and personate the second son of Edward the Fourth, supposed to be murdered, and afterward (for he changed his intention in the manage) the Lord Edward Plantagenet, then prisoner in the Tower, and accordingly to frame him and instruct him in the part he was to play. This is that which (as was touched before) seems scarcely credible; not that a false person should be assumed to gain a kingdom, for it has been seen in ancient and late times; nor that it should come into the mind of such an abject fellow to enterprise so great a matter, for high conceits do sometimes come streaming into the imaginations of base persons, especially when they are drunk with news and talk of the people. But here is that which has no appearance; that this priest, being utterly unacquainted with the true person according to whose pattern he should shape his counterfeit, should think it possible for him to instruct his player, either in gesture and fashions, or in recounting past matters of his life and education, or in fit answers to questions, or the like, any ways to come near the resemblance of him whom he was to represent. For this lad was not to personate one that had been long before taken out of his cradle, or conveyed away in his infancy, known to few, but a youth that till the age almost of ten years had been brought up in a court where infinite eyes had been upon him. For King Edward, touched with remorse of his brother the Duke of Clarence's death, would not indeed restore his son (of whom we speak) to be Duke of Clarence, but yet created him Earl of Warwick, reviving his honour on the mother's side, and used him honourably during his time, though Richard the Third afterwards confined him. So that it cannot be, but that some great person, that knew particularly and familiarly Edward Plantagenet, had a hand in the business, from whom the priest might take his aim.

That which is most probable, out of the precedent and subsequent acts, is, that it was the Queen Dowager[40] from whom this action had the principal source and motion. For certain it is, she was a busy negotiating woman, and in her withdrawing-chamber had the fortunate conspiracy for the King against King Richard the Third been hatched, which the King knew, and remembered perhaps but too well; and she was at this time extremely discontent with the King, thinking her daughter (as the King handled the matter) not advanced but depressed, and none could hold the book so well to prompt and instruct this stage play, as she could. Nevertheless it was not her meaning, nor no more was it the meaning of any of the better and sager sort that favoured this enterprise and knew the secret, that this disguised idol should possess the crown; but at his peril to make way to the overthrow of the King, and that done, they had their several hopes and ways.

That which does chiefly fortify this conjecture is, that as soon as the matter broke forth in any strength, it was one of the King's first acts to cloister the Queen Dowager in the nunnery of Bermondsey, and to take away all her lands and estate, and this by a close council, without any legal proceeding, upon far-fetched pretences – that she had delivered her two daughters out of sanctuary to King Richard, contrary to promise. Which proceeding being even at that time taxed for rigorous and undue, both in matter and manner, makes it very probable there was some greater matter against her, which the King upon reason of policy and to avoid envy would not publish. It is likewise no small argument that there was some secret in it and some suppressing of examinations, for that the priest Simons himself after he was taken was never brought to execution; no, not so much as to public trial (as many clergymen were upon less treasons), but was only shut up close in a dungeon. Add to this that after the Earl of Lincoln (a principal person of the house of York) was slain in Stokefield, the King opened himself to some of his council, that he was sorry for the Earl's death, because by him (he said) he might have known the bottom of his danger.

But to return to the narration itself. Simons did first instruct his scholar for the part of Richard Duke of York, second son to King Edward the Fourth; and this was at such time as it was voiced that the King purposed to put to death Edward Plantagenet, prisoner in the Tower, whereat there was great murmur. But hearing soon after a general bruit that Plantagenet had escaped out of the Tower, and thereby finding him so much beloved amongst the people, and such rejoicing at his escape, the cunning priest changed his copy and chose now Plantagenet to be the subject his pupil should personate, because he was more in the present speech and votes of the people, and it pieced better, and followed more close and handsomely upon the bruit of Plantagenet's escape. But yet doubting that there would be too near looking and too much perspective into his disguise, if he should show it here in England, he thought good (after the manner of scenes in stage plays and masques) to show it afar off, and therefore sailed with his scholar into Ireland, where the affection to the house of York was most in height. The King had been a little improvident in the matters of Ireland, and had not removed officers and counsellors, and put in their places, or at least intermingled, persons of whom he stood assured, as he should have done, since he knew the strong bent of that country towards the house of York, and that it was a ticklish and unsettled state, more easy to receive distempers and mutations than England was. But trusting to the reputation of his victories and successes in England, he thought he should have time enough to extend his cares afterwards to that second kingdom.

Wherefore through this neglect, upon the coming of Simons with his pretended Plantagenet into Ireland, all things were prepared for revolt and sedition, almost as if they had been set and plotted beforehand. Simons' first address was to the Lord Thomas Fitzgerald, Earl of Kildare and Deputy of Ireland, before whose eyes he did cast such a mist (by his own insinuation, and by the carriage of his youth, which expressed a natural princely behaviour) as, joined perhaps with some inward vapours of ambition and affection in the Earl's own mind, left him fully possessed that it was the true Plantagenet. The Earl presently communicated the matter with some of the nobles and others there, at the first secretly. But finding them of like affection to himself, he suffered it of purpose to vent and pass abroad, because they thought it not safe to resolve, till they had a taste of the people's inclination. But if the great ones were in forwardness, the people were in fury, entertaining this airy body or phantasm with incredible affection, partly out of their great devotion to the house of York, partly out of a proud humour in the nation to give a king to the realm of England. Neither did the party in this heat of affection much trouble themselves with the attainder of George Duke of Clarence, having newly learned by the King's example that attainders do not interrupt the conveying of title to the crown. And as for the daughters of King Edward the Fourth, they thought King Richard had said enough for them, and took them to be but as of the King's party, because they were in his power and at his disposing. So that with marvellous consent and applause, this counterfeit Plantagenet was brought with great solemnity to the castle of Dublin, and there saluted, served, and honoured as king, the boy becoming it well, and doing nothing that did bewray the baseness of his condition. And within a few days after he was proclaimed king in Dublin, by the name of King Edward the Sixth, there being not a sword drawn in King Henry his quarrel.[41]

The King was much moved with this unexpected accident when it came to his ears, both because it struck upon that string that ever he most feared, as also because it was stirred in such a place where he could not with safety transfer his own person to suppress it. For partly through natural valour and partly through a universal suspicion (not knowing whom to trust) he was ever ready to wait upon all his achievements in person. The King therefore first called his council together at the Charter-house at Sheen,[42] which council was held with great secrecy, but the open decrees thereof, which presently came abroad, were three.

The first was, that the Queen Dowager, for that she, contrary to her pact and agreement with those that had concluded with her concerning the marriage of her daughter Elizabeth with King Henry, had nevertheless delivered her daughters out of sanctuary into King Richard's hands, should be cloistered in the nunnery of Bermondsey, and forfeit all her lands and goods.

The next was, that Edward Plantagenet, then close prisoner in the Tower, should be, in the most public and notorious manner that could be devised, showed unto the people: in part to discharge the King of the envy of that opinion and bruit, how he had been put to death privily in the Tower, but chiefly to make the people see the levity and imposture of the proceedings of Ireland, and that their Plantagenet was indeed but a puppet or a counterfeit.

The third was, that there should be again proclaimed a general pardon to all that would reveal their offences and submit themselves by a day, and that this pardon should be conceived in so ample and liberal a manner as no high treason (no not against the King's own person) should be excepted. Which though it might seem strange, yet was it not so to a wise king, that knew his greatest dangers were not from the least treasons, but from the greatest. These resolutions of the King and his council were immediately put in execution. And first, the Queen Dowager was put into the monastery of Bermondsey, and all her estate seized into the King's hands: whereat there was much wondering, that a weak woman, for the yielding to the menaces and promises of a tyrant, after such a distance of time (wherein the King had shown no displeasure nor alteration), but much more after so happy a marriage between the King and her daughter, blessed with issue male, should upon a sudden mutability or disclosure of the King's mind be so severely handled.

This lady was amongst the examples of great variety of fortune. She had first, from a distressed suitor[43] and desolate widow, been taken to the marriage bed of a bachelor-king, the goodliest personage of his time, and even in his reign she had endured a strange eclipse, by the King's flight and temporary depriving from the crown. She was also very happy in that she had by him fair issue, and continued his nuptial love (helping herself by some obsequious bearing and dissembling of his pleasures) to the very end. She was much affectionate to her own kindred, even unto faction, which did stir great envy in the lords of the King's side, who counted her blood a disparagement to be mingled with the King's. With which lords of the King's blood joined also the King's favourite the Lord Hastings, who, notwithstanding the King's great affection to him, was thought at times, through her malice and spleen, not to be out of danger of falling. After her husband's death she was matter of tragedy, having lived to see her brother beheaded, and her two sons deposed from the crown, bastarded in their blood,[44] and cruelly murdered. All this while nevertheless she enjoyed her liberty, state, and fortunes. But afterwards again, upon the rise of the wheel, when she had a king to her son-in-law, and was made grandmother to a grandchild of the best sex, yet was she (upon dark and unknown reasons, and no less strange pretences) precipitated and banished the world into a nunnery; where it was almost thought dangerous to visit her or see her, and where not long after she ended her life, but was by the King's commandment buried with the King her husband at Windsor. She was foundress of Queen's College[45] in Cambridge. For this act the King sustained great obloquy, which nevertheless (besides the reason of state) was somewhat sweetened him by a great confiscation.[46]

About this time also, Edward Plantagenet was upon a Sunday brought throughout all the principal streets of London, to be seen of the people. And having passed the view of the streets, was conducted to Paul's Church in solemn procession, where great store of people were assembled. And it was provided also in good fashion, that divers of the nobility and others of quality (especially of those that the King most suspected, and knew the person of Plantagenet best) had communication with the young gentleman by the way, and entertained him with speech and discourse, which did in effect mar the pageant in Ireland with the subjects here, at least with so many as out of error, and not out of malice, might be misled. Nevertheless in Ireland (where it was too late to go back) it wrought little or no effect. But contrariwise they turned the imposture upon the King, and gave out that the King, to defeat the true inheritor, and to mock the world and blind the eyes of simple men, had tricked up a boy in the likeness of Edward Plantagenet, and showed him to the people, not sparing to profane the ceremony of a procession, the more to countenance the fable.

The general pardon likewise near the same time came forth, and the King therewithal omitted no diligence in giving straight order for the keeping of the ports, that fugitives, malcontents, or suspected persons might not pass over into Ireland and Flanders.

Meanwhile the rebels in Ireland had sent privy messengers both into England and into Flanders, who in both places had wrought effects of no small importance. For in England they won to their party John Earl of Lincoln, son of John de la Pole, Duke of Suffolk, and of Elizabeth, King Edward the Fourth's eldest sister. This earl was a man of great wit and courage, and had his thoughts highly raised by hopes and expectations for a time. For Richard the Third had a resolution, out of his hatred to both his brethren, King Edward and the Duke of Clarence, and their lines (having had his hand in both their bloods), to disable their issues upon false and incompetent pretexts, the one of attainder, the other of illegitimation; and to design this gentleman (in case himself should die without children) for inheritor of the crown. Neither was this unknown to the King (who had secretly an eye upon him), but the King having tasted of the envy of the people for his imprisonment of Edward Plantagenet, was doubtful to heap up any more distastes of that kind by the imprisonment of de la Pole also, the rather thinking it policy to conserve him as a co-rival unto the other. The Earl of Lincoln was induced to participate with the action of Ireland, not lightly upon the strength of the proceedings there, which was but a bubble, but upon letters from the Lady Margaret of Burgundy, in whose succours and declaration for the enterprise there seemed to be a more solid foundation, both for reputation and forces. Neither did the Earl refrain the business for that he knew pretended Plantagenet to be but an idol. But contrariwise he was more glad it should be the false Plantagenet than the true, because the false being sure to fall away of himself, and the true to be made sure of by the King, it might open and pave a fair and prepared way to his own title. With this resolution he sailed secretly into Flanders, where was a little before arrived the Lord Lovel, leaving a correspondence here in England with Sir Thomas Broughton, a man of great power and dependencies in Lancashire.

For before this time, when the pretended Plantagenet was first received in Ireland, secret messengers had been also sent to the Lady Margaret, advertising her what had passed in Ireland, imploring succours in an enterprise (as they said) so pious and just, and that God had so miraculously prospered in the beginning thereof, and making offer that all things should be guided by her will and direction, as the sovereign patroness and protectress of the enterprise. Margaret was second sister to King Edward the Fourth, and had been second wife to Charles surnamed the Hardy, Duke of Burgundy. By whom having no children of her own, she did with singular care and tenderness intend the education of Philip and Margaret, grandchildren to her former husband, which won her great love and authority among the Dutch. This princess (having the spirit of a man and malice of a woman) abounding in treasure by the greatness of her dower and her provident government, and being childless and without any nearer care, made it her design and enterprise to see the majesty royal of England once again replaced in her house, and had set up King Henry as a mark at whose overthrow all her actions should aim and shoot, insomuch as all the counsels of his succeeding troubles came chiefly out of that quiver. And she bore such a mortal hatred to the house of Lancaster and personally to the King, as she was no ways mollified by the conjunction of the houses in her niece's marriage, but rather hated her niece, as the means of the King's ascent to the crown and assurance therein. Wherefore with great violence of affection she embraced this overture.

And upon counsel taken with the Earl of Lincoln and the Lord Lovel, and some other of the party, it was resolved with all speed, the two lords assisted with a regiment of 2,000 Almains, being choice and veteran bands, under the command of Martin Swart (a valiant and experimented captain) should pass over into Ireland to the new king, hoping that when the action should have the face of a received and settled regality (with such a second person as the Earl of Lincoln, and the conjunction and reputation of foreign succours), the fame of it would embolden and prepare all the party of the confederates and malcontents within the realm of England to give them assistance when they should come over there. And for the person of the counterfeit, it was agreed that if all things succeeded well he should be put down, and the true Plantagenet received, wherein nevertheless the Earl of Lincoln had his particular hopes.

After they were come into Ireland (and that the party took courage by seeing themselves together in a body) they grew very confident of success, conceiving and discoursing amongst themselves, that they went in upon far better cards to overthrow King Henry, than King Henry had to overthrow King Richard, and that if there were not a sword drawn against them in Ireland, it was a sign the swords in England would be soon sheathed or beaten down. And first, for a bravery upon this accession of power, they crowned their new king in the cathedral church of Dublin, who formerly had been but proclaimed only, and then sat in council what should further be done. At which council though it were propounded by some that it were the best way to establish themselves first in Ireland to make that the seat of the war, and to draw King Henry thither in person, by whose absence they thought there would be alterations and commotions in England; yet because the kingdom there was poor, and they should not be able to keep their army together, nor pay their German soldiers, and for that also the sway of the Irishmen and generally of the men of war, which (as in such cases of popular tumults is usual) did in effect govern their leaders, was eager and in affection to make their fortunes upon England; it was concluded with all possible speed to transport their forces into England.

The King in the meantime, who at the first when he heard what was done in Ireland, though it troubled him, yet thought he should be well enough able to scatter the Irish as a flight of birds, and rattle away this swarm of bees with their king; when he heard afterwards that the Earl of Lincoln was embarked in the action, and that the Lady Margaret was declared for it, he apprehended the danger in a true degree as it was, and saw plainly that his kingdom must again be put to the stake, and that he must fight for it. And first he did conceive, before he understood of the Earl of Lincoln's sailing into Ireland out of Flanders, that he should be assailed both upon the east parts of the kingdom of England by some impression from Flanders, and upon the northwest out of Ireland: and therefore having ordered musters to be made in both parts, and having provisionally designed two generals, Jasper Earl of Bedford, and John Earl of Oxford (meaning himself also to go in person where the affairs should most require it), and nevertheless not expecting any actual invasion at that time, the winter being far on, he took his journey himself towards Suffolk and Norfolk, for the confirming of those parts. And being come to St Edmondsbury, he understood that Thomas Marquis of Dorset (who had been one of the pledges in France) was hasting towards him to purge himself of some accusations that had been made against him. But the King, though he kept an ear for[47] him, yet was the time so doubtful that he sent the Earl of Oxford to meet him and forthwith to carry him to the Tower, with a fair message nevertheless that he should bear that disgrace with patience, for that the King meant not his hurt, but only to preserve him from doing hurt either to the King's service or to himself, and that the King should always be able (when he had cleared himself) to make him reparation.

From St Edmondsbury he went to Norwich, where he kept his Christmas. And from thence he went (in a manner of pilgrimage) to Walsingham, where he visited our Lady's church, famous for miracles, and made his prayers and vows for his help and deliverance. And from thence he returned by Cambridge to London. Not long after, the rebels with their king (under the leading of the Earl of Lincoln, the Earl of Kildare, the Lord Lovel, and Colonel Swart) landed at Fouldrey in Lancashire, whither there repaired to them Sir Thomas Broughton, with some small company of English. The King by that time (knowing now the storm would not divide but fall in one place) had levied forces in good number, and in person (taking with him his two designed generals, the Duke of Bedford and the Earl of Oxford) was come on his way towards them as far as Coventry, whence he sent forth a troop of light horsemen for discovery, and to intercept some stragglers of the enemies, by whom he might the better understand the particulars of their progress and purposes, which was accordingly done, though the King otherways was not without intelligence from espials in the camp.

The rebels took their way towards York without spoiling the country or any act of hostility, the better to put themselves into favour of the people and to personate their king[48] (who no doubt out of a princely feeling was sparing and compassionate towards his subjects). But their snowball did not gather as it went. For the people came not in to them, neither did any rise or declare themselves in other parts of the kingdom for them, which was caused partly by the good taste that the King had given his people of his government, joined with the reputation of his felicity, and partly for that it was an odious thing to the people of England to have a king brought in to them upon the shoulders of Irish and Dutch, of which their army was in substance compounded. Neither was it a thing done with any great judgement on the party of the rebels, for them to take their way towards York, considering that howsoever those parts had formerly been a nursery of their friends, yet it was there where the Lord Lovel had so lately disbanded, and where the King's presence had a little before qualified discontents. The Earl of Lincoln, deceived of his hopes of the country's concourse unto him (in which case he would have temporised) and seeing the business past retreat, resolved to make on where the King was, and to give him battle, and thereupon marched toward Newark, thinking to have surprised the town. But the King was somewhat before this time come to Nottingham, where he called a council of war, at which was consulted whether it were best to protract time or speedily to set upon the rebels. In which council the King himself (whose continual vigilance did suck in sometimes causeless suspicions that few else knew) inclined to the accelerating a battle. But this was presently put out of doubt, by the great aids that came in to him in the instant of this consultation, partly upon missives and partly voluntaries from many parts of the kingdom.

The principal persons that came then to the King's aid were the Earl of Shrewsbury and the Lord Strange, of the nobility, and of knights and gentlemen to the number of at least three-score and ten persons, with their companies, making in the whole at the least 6,000 fighting men, besides the forces that were with the King before. Whereupon the King, finding his army so bravely reinforced, and a great alacrity in all his men to fight, he was confirmed in his former resolution, and marched speedily, so as he put himself between the enemies' camp and Newark, being loath their army should get the commodity of that town. The Earl, nothing dismayed, came forwards that day unto a little village called Stoke, and there encamped that night, upon the brow or hanging of a hill. The King the next day presented him battle upon the plain (the fields there being open and champaign). The Earl courageously came down and joined battle with him.

Concerning which battle the relations that are left unto us are so naked and negligent (though it be an action of so recent memory) as they rather declare the success of the day than the manner of the fight. They say that the King divided his army into three battles, whereof the vanguard only, well strengthened with wings, came to fight; that the fight was fierce and obstinate, and lasted three hours before the victory inclined either way, save that judgement might be made by that the King's vanguard of itself maintained fight against the whole power of the enemies (the other two battles remaining out of action), what the success was like to be in the end; that Martin Swart with his Germans performed bravely, and so did those few English that were on that side; neither did the Irish fail in courage or fierceness, but being almost naked men, only armed with darts and skeins, it was rather an execution than a fight upon them, insomuch as the furious slaughter of them was a great couragement and appalment to the rest; that there died upon the place all the chieftains, that is, the Earl of Lincoln, the Earl of Kildare, Francis Lord Lovel, Martin Swart, and Sir Thomas Broughton, all making good the fight without any ground given. Only of the Lord Lovel there went a report that he fled, and swam over Trent on horseback, but could not recover the further side, by reason of the steepness of the bank, and so was drowned in the river. But another report leaves him not there, but that he lived long after in a cave or vault. The number that was slain in the field was of the enemies' part 4,000 at the least, and of the King's part one half of his vanguard, besides many hurt, but none of name. There were taken prisoners amongst others the counterfeit Plantagenet, now Lambert Simnel again, and the crafty priest his tutor. For Lambert, the King would not take his life, both out of magnanimity (taking him but as an image of wax that others had tempered and moulded), and likewise out of wisdom, thinking that if he suffered death he would be forgotten too soon, but being kept alive he would be a continual spectacle, and a kind of remedy against the like enchantments of people in time to come. For which cause he was taken into service in his court to a base office in his kitchen, so that (in a kind of *mattacina* of human fortune) he turned a broach that had worn a crown, whereas fortune commonly does not bring in a comedy or farce after a tragedy. And afterwards he was preferred to be one of the King's falconers. As to the priest, he was committed close prisoner, and heard of no more, the King loving to seal up his own dangers.

After the battle the King went to Lincoln, where he caused supplications and thanksgivings to be made for his deliverance and victory. And that his devotions might go round in circle, he sent his banner to be offered to our Lady of Walsingham, where before he made his vows.

And thus delivered of this so strange an engine and new invention of fortune, he returned to his former confidence of mind, thinking now that all his misfortunes had come at once. But it fell unto him according to the speech of the common people in the beginning of his reign, that said, 'It was a token he should reign in labour, because his reign began with a sickness of sweat.' But howsoever the King thought himself now in the haven, yet such was his wisdom as his confidence did seldom darken his foresight, especially in things near hand, and therefore, awakened by so fresh and unexpected dangers, he entered into due consideration as well how to weed out the partakers of the former rebellion, as to kill the seeds the like in time to come, and withal to take away all shelters and harbours for discontented persons, where they might hatch and foster rebellions that afterwards might gather strength and motion.

And first he did yet again make a progress from Lincoln to the northern parts, though it were (indeed) rather an itinerary circuit of justice than a progress. For all along as he went, with much severity and strict inquisition, partly by martial law and partly by commission, were punished the adherents and aiders of the late rebels: not all by death (for the field had drawn much blood), but by fines and ransoms, which spared life and raised treasure. Amongst other crimes of this nature, there was a diligent inquiry made of such as had raised and dispersed a bruit and rumour (a little before the field fought), that the rebels had the day and that the King's army was overthrown, and the King fled, whereby it was supposed that many succours that otherwise would have come unto the King were cunningly put off and kept back, which charge and accusation, though it had some ground, yet it was industriously embraced and put on by divers, who (having been in themselves not the best affected to the King's part, nor forward to come to his aid) were glad to apprehend this colour to cover their neglect and coldness under the pretence of such discouragements. Which cunning nevertheless the King would not understand,[49] though he lodged it and noted it in some particulars, as his manner was.

But for the extirpating of the roots and causes of the like commotions in time to come, the King began to find where his shoe did wring him, and that it was his depressing of the house of York that did rankle and fester the affections of his people. And therefore, being now too wise to disdain perils any longer, and willing to give some contentment in that kind (at least in ceremony), he resolved at last to proceed to the coronation of his queen. And therefore, at his coming to London, where he entered in state and in a kind of triumph, and celebrated his victory with two days of devotion (for the first day he repaired to Paul's, and had the hymn of *Te Deum* sung, and the morrow after he went in procession, and heard the sermon at the Cross[50]), the Queen was with great solemnity crowned at Westminster, the twenty-fifth of November, in the third year of his reign, which was about two years after the marriage (like an old christening that had stayed long for godfathers), which strange and unusual distance of time made it subject to every man's note that it was an act against his stomach, and put upon him by necessity and reason of state. Soon after, to show that it was now fair weather again, and that the imprisonment of Thomas Marquis Dorset was rather upon suspicion of the time than of the man, he, the said Marquis, was set at liberty, without examination or other circumstance.

At that time also the King sent an ambassador unto Pope Innocent,[51] signifying unto him this his marriage, and that now like another Aeneas[52] he had passed through the floods of his former troubles and travails and was arrived unto a safe haven, and thanking his Holiness that he had honoured the celebration of his marriage with the presence of his ambassador, and offering both his person and the forces of his kingdom upon all occasions to do him service.

The ambassador, making his oration to the Pope in the presence of the cardinals, did so magnify the King and Queen as was enough to glut the hearers. But then he did again so extol and deify the Pope as made all that he had said in praise of his master and mistress seem temperate and passable. But he was very honourably entertained and extremely much made on by the Pope, who knowing himself to be lazy and unprofitable to the Christian world, was wonderful glad to hear that there were such echoes of him sounding in remote parts. He obtained also of the Pope a very just and honourable bull, qualifying the privileges of sanctuary (wherewith the King had been extremely galled) in three points.

The first, that if any sanctuary man did by night or otherwise get out of sanctuary privily and commit mischief and trespass, and then come in again, he should lose the benefit of sanctuary for ever after.

The second, that howsoever the person of the sanctuary man was protected from his creditors, yet his goods out of sanctuary should not.

The third, that if any took sanctuary for case of treason, the King might appoint him keepers to look to him in sanctuary.

The King also, for the better securing of his estate against mutinous and malcontented subjects (whereof he saw the realm was full) who might have their refuge into Scotland (which was not under key as the ports were), for that cause, rather than for any doubt of hostility from those parts, before his coming to London, when he was at Newcastle, had sent a solemn ambassage unto James the Third, King of Scotland, to treat and conclude a peace with him. The ambassadors were Richard Fox, Bishop of Exeter, and Sir Richard Edgcombe, comptroller of the King's house, who were honourably received and entertained there. But the King of Scotland, labouring of the same disease that King Henry did (though more mortal as afterwards appeared), that is, discontented subjects to rise and raise tumult, although in his own affection he did much desire to make a peace with the King, yet finding his nobles averse and not daring to displease them, concluded only a truce for seven years, giving nevertheless promise in private that it should be renewed from time to time during the two kings' lives.

Hitherto the King had been exercised in settling his affairs at home. But about this time broke forth an occasion that drew him to look abroad and to hearken to foreign business. Charles the Eighth, the French King, by the virtue and good fortune of his two immediate predecessors, Charles the Seventh his grandfather and Lewis the Eleventh his father, received the kingdom of France in more flourishing and spread estate than it had been of many years before; being redintegrate in[53] those principal members that anciently had been portions of the crown of France, and were after disseuered, so as they remained only in homage and not in sovereignty, being governed by absolute princes of their own: Anjou, Normandy, Provence, and Burgundy. There remained only Brittany to be reunited, and so the monarchy of France to be reduced to the ancient terms and bounds.

King Charles was not a little inflamed with an ambition to repurchase and reannex that duchy, which his ambition was a wise and well-weighed ambition, not like unto the ambitions of his succeeding enterprises of Italy. For at that time, being newly come to the crown, he was somewhat guided by his father's counsels (counsels not counsellors, for his father was his own counsel, and had few able men about him); and that king (he knew well) had ever distasted the designs of Italy, and in particular had an eye upon Brittany. There were many circumstances that did feed the ambition of Charles with pregnant and apparent hopes of success: the Duke of Brittany old, and entered into a lethargy, and served with mercenary counsellors, father of two only daughters, the one sickly and not like to continue; King Charles himself in the flower of his age, and the subjects of France at that time well trained for war, both for leaders and soldiers (men of service being not yet worn out since the wars of Lewis against Burgundy). He found himself also in peace with all his neighbour princes. As for those that might oppose to his enterprise: Maximilian, King of the Romans, his rival in the same desires (as well for the duchy as the daughter), feeble in means; and King Henry of England, as well somewhat obnoxious to him for his favours and benefits, as busied in his particular troubles at home. There was also a fair and specious occasion offered him to hide his ambition and to justify his warring upon Brittany, for that the Duke had received and succoured Lewis Duke of Orleans and others of the French nobility, which had taken arms against their King.

Wherefore King Charles, being resolved upon that war, knew well he could not receive any opposition so potent as if King Henry should either upon policy of state in preventing the growing greatness of France, or upon gratitude unto the Duke of Brittany for his former favours in the time of his distress,[54] espouse that quarrel and declare himself in aid of the Duke. Therefore he no sooner heard that King Henry was settled by his victory, but forthwith he sent ambassadors unto him to pray his assistance, or at least that he would stand neutral. Which ambassadors found the King at Leicester and delivered their ambassage to this effect. They first imparted unto the King the success that their master had had a little before against Maximilian in recovery of certain towns from him, which done in a kind of privacy and inwardness towards the King, as if the French King did not esteem him for an outward or formal confederate, but as one that had part in his affections and fortunes, and with whom he took pleasure to communicate his business.

After this compliment and some gratulation for the King's victory they fell to their errand: declaring to the King that their master was enforced to enter into a just and necessary war with the Duke of Brittany, for that he had received and succoured those that were traitors and declared enemies unto his person and state; that they were no mean distressed and calamitous persons that fled to him for refuge, but of so great quality as it was apparent that they came not thither to protect their own fortune, but to infest and invade his; the head of them being the Duke of Orleans, the first prince of the blood and the second person of France. That therefore rightly to understand it, it was rather on their master's part a defensive war than an offensive, as that that could not be omitted or forborne if he tendered the conservation of his own estate, and that it was not the first blow that made the war invasive (for that no wise prince would stay for), but the first provocation, or at least the first preparation; nay that this war was rather a suppression of rebels than a war with a just enemy, where the case is, that his subjects traitors are received by the Duke of Brittany his homager. That King Henry knew well what went upon it in example, if neighbour princes should patronise and comfort rebels against the law of nations and of leagues; nevertheless that their master was not ignorant that the King had been beholding to the Duke of Brittany in his adversity, as on the other side they knew he would not forget also the readiness of their king in aiding him when the Duke of Brittany or his mercenary counsellors failed him, and would have betrayed him, and that there was a great difference between the courtesies received from their master and the Duke of Brittany, for that the Duke's might have ends of utility and bargain, whereas their master's could not have proceeded but out of entire affection, for that if it had been measured by a politic line, it had been better for his affairs that a tyrant should have reigned in England, troubled and hated, than such a prince whose virtues could not fail to make him great and potent, whensoever he was come to be master of his affairs. But howsoever it stood for the point of obligation that the King might owe to the Duke of Brittany, yet their master was well assured it would not divert King Henry of England from doing that that was just, nor ever embark him in so ill-grounded a quarrel.

Therefore since this war that their master was now to make was but to deliver himself from imminent dangers, their king hoped the King would show the like affection to the conservation of their master's estate, as their master had (when time was) showed to the King's acquisition of his kingdom. At the least that, according to the inclination that the King had ever professed of peace, he would look on and stand neutral, for that their master could not with reason press him to undertake part in the war, being so newly settled and recovered from intestine seditions. But touching the mystery of reannexing of the duchy of Brittany to the crown of France, either by war or by marriage with the daughter of Brittany, the ambassadors bore aloof from it as from a rock, knowing that it made most against them, and therefore by all means declined any mention thereof, but contrariwise interlaced in their conference with the King the assured purpose of their master to match with the daughter of Maximilian, and entertained the King also with some wandering discourses of their king's purpose to recover by arms his right to the kingdom of Naples, by an expedition in person; all to remove the King from all jealousy of any design in these hither parts upon Brittany,[55] otherwise than for quenching of the fire that he feared might be kindled in his own estate.

The King, after advice taken with his council, made answer to the ambassadors. And first returned their compliment, showing he was right glad of the French King's reception of those towns from Maximilian. Then he familiarly related some particular passages of his own adventures and victory passed. As to the business of Brittany, the King answered in few words, that the French King and the Duke of Brittany were the two persons to whom he was most obliged of all men, and that he should think himself very unhappy if things should go so between them as he should not be able to acquit himself in gratitude towards them both, and that there was no means for him, as a Christian king and a common friend to them, to satisfy all obligations both to God and man, but to offer himself for a mediator of an accord and peace between them, by which course he doubted not but their king's estate and honour both would be preserved with more safety and less envy than by a war, and that he would spare no cost or pains, no if it were to go on pilgrimage,[56] for so good an effect; and concluded that in this great affair, which he took so much to heart, he would express himself more fully by an ambassage, which he would speedily despatch unto the French King for that purpose. And in this sort the French ambassadors were dismissed, the King avoiding to understand anything touching the reannexing of Brittany, as the ambassadors had avoided to mention it, save that he gave a little touch of it in the word 'envy'. And so it was that the King was neither so shallow nor so ill advertised as not to perceive the intention of the French for the investing himself of Brittany. But first, he was utterly unwilling (howsoever he gave out) to enter into a war with France. A fame of a war he liked well, but not an achievement; for the one he thought would make him richer, and the other poorer; and he was possessed with many secret fears touching his own people, which he was therefore loath to arm, and put weapons into their hands. Yet notwithstanding, as a prudent and courageous prince, he was not so averse from a war, but that he was resolved to choose it rather than to have Brittany carried by France, being so great and opulent a duchy, and situate so opportunely to annoy England, either for coast or trade. But the King's hopes were, that partly by negligence, commonly imputed to the French (especially in the court of a young king), and partly by the native power of Brittany itself, which was not small, but chiefly in respect of the great party that the Duke of Orleans had in the kingdom of France, and thereby means to stir up civil troubles to divert the French King from the enterprise of Brittany, and lastly in regard of the power of Maximilian, who was co-rival to the French King in the pursuit, the enterprise would either bow to a peace or break in itself. In all which the King measured and valued things amiss, as afterwards appeared.

He sent therefore forthwith to the French King, Christopher Urswick his chaplain, a person by him much trusted and employed, choosing him the rather because he was a churchman, as best sorting with an embassy of pacification, and giving him also a commission that if the French King consented to treat, he should thence repair to the Duke of Brittany and ripen the treaty on both parts. Urswick made declaration to the French King much to the purpose of the King's answer to the French ambassadors here, instilling also tenderly some overture of receiving to grace the Duke of Orleans, and some taste of conditions of accord. But the French King on the other side proceeded not sincerely, but with a great deal of art and dissimulation in this treaty, having for his end to gain time, and so put off the English succours, under hope of peace, till he had got good footing in Brittany by force of arms. Wherefore he answered the ambassador, that he would put himself into the King's hands, and make him arbiter of the peace, and willingly consented that the ambassadors should straightways pass into Brittany to signify this his consent, and to know the Duke's mind likewise, well foreseeing that the Duke of Orleans, by whom the Duke of Brittany was wholly led, taking himself to be upon terms irreconcileable with him, would admit of no treaty of peace; whereby he should in one both generally abroad veil over his ambition, and win the reputation of just and moderate proceedings, and should withal endear himself in the affections of the King of England, as one that had committed all to his will, nay and (which was yet more fine) make faith in him that although he went on with the war, yet it should be but with his sword in his hand to bend the stiffness of the other party to accept of peace, and so the King should take no umbrage of his arming and prosecution, but the treaty to be kept on foot to the very last instant, till he were master of the field. Which grounds being by the French King wisely laid, all things fell out as he expected. For when the English ambassador came to the court of Brittany, the Duke was then scarcely perfect[57] in his memory, and all things were directed by the Duke of Orleans, who gave audience to the chaplain Urswick, and upon his ambassage delivered made answer in somewhat high terms: that the Duke of Brittany having been a host and a kind of parent or foster father to the King in his tenderness of age and weakness of fortune, did look for at this time from King Henry (the renowned King of England) rather brave troops for his succours than a vain treaty of peace. And if the King could forget the good offices of the Duke done unto him aforetime, yet he knew well he would in his wisdom consider of the future, how much it imported his own safety and reputation both in foreign parts and with his own people, not to suffer Brittany (the old confederates of England) to be swallowed up by France, and so many good ports and strong towns upon the coast be in the command of so potent a neighbour king and so ancient an enemy, and therefore humbly desired the King to think of this business as his own: and therewith broke off, and denied any further conference for treaty.

Urswick returned first to the French King, and related to him what had passed. Who, finding things to sort to his desire, took hold of them, and said, that the ambassador might perceive now that which he for his part partly imagined before, that considering in what hands the Duke of Brittany was, there would be no peace but by a mixed treaty of force and persuasion, and therefore he would go on with the one, and desired the King not to desist from the other; but for his own part, he did faithfully promise to be still in the King's power, to rule him in the matter of peace. This was accordingly represented unto the King by Urswick at his return, and in such a fashion as if the treaty were in no sort desperate, but rather stayed for a better hour, till the hammer had wrought and beat the party of Brittany more pliant, whereupon there passed continually packets and despatches between the two kings, from the one out of desire, and from the other out of dissimulation about the negotiation of peace.

The French King meanwhile invaded Brittany with great forces, and distressed the city of Nantes with a strait siege, and (as one who, though he had no great judgement, yet had that, that he could dissemble home) the more he did urge the prosecution of the war, the more he did at the same time urge the solicitation of the peace, insomuch as during the siege of Nantes, after many letters and particular messages, the better to maintain his dissimulation and to refresh the treaty, he sent Bernard Daubigney, a person of good quality, to the King, earnestly to desire him to make an end of the business howsoever. The King was no less ready to revive and quicken the treaty, and thereupon sent three commissioners, the Abbot of Abingdon, Sir Richard Tunstall, and Chaplain Urswick formerly employed, to do their utmost endeavour to manage the treaty roundly and strongly.

About this time the Lord Woodville (uncle to the Queen), a valiant gentleman and desirous of honour, sued to the King that he might raise some power of voluntaries underhand, and without licence or passport (wherein the King might any ways appear) go to the aid of the Duke of Brittany. The King denied his request, or at least seemed so to do, and laid strait commandment upon him that he should not stir, for that the King thought his honour would suffer therein, during a treaty to better a party. Nevertheless this lord (either being unruly, or out of conceit that the King would not inwardly dislike that which he would not openly avow), sailed secretly over into the Isle of Wight, whereof he was governor, and levied a fair troop of 400 men, and with them passed over into Brittany and joined himself with the Duke's forces. The news whereof, when it came to the French court, put divers young bloods into such a fury as the English ambassadors were not without peril to be outraged. But the French King, both to preserve the privilege of ambassadors, and being conscious to himself that in the business of peace he himself was the greater dissembler of the two, forbad all injuries of fact or word against their persons or followers. And presently came an agent from the King to purge himself touching the Lord Woodville's going over, using for a principal argument to demonstrate that it was without his privity, for that the troops were so small as neither had the face of a succour by authority, nor could much advance the Breton affairs. To which message, although the French King gave no full credit, yet he made fair weather with the King, and seemed satisfied.

Soon after the English ambassadors returned, having two of them been likewise with the Duke of Brittany and found things in no other terms than they were before. Upon their return they informed the King of the state of the affairs, and how far the French King was from any true meaning of peace, and therefore he was now to advise of some other course. Neither was the King himself led all this while with credulity merely, as was generally supposed. But his error was not so much facility of belief as an ill-measuring of the forces of the other party. For (as was partly touched before) the King had cast the business thus with himself. He took it for granted in his own judgement that the war of Brittany, in respect of the strength of the towns and of the party, could not speedily come to a period. For he conceived that the councils of a war that was undertaken by the French King (then childless) against an heir apparent[58] of France, would be very faint and slow, and besides, that it was not possible but that the state of France should be embroiled with some troubles and alterations in favour of the Duke of Orleans. He conceived likewise that Maximilian, King of the Romans, was a prince warlike and potent, who he made account would give succours to the Bretons roundly. So then, judging it would be a work of time, he laid his plot how he might best make use of that time for his own affairs. Wherein first he thought to make his vantage upon his parliament, knowing that they being affectionate unto the quarrel of Brittany would give treasure largely. Which treasure, as a noise of war might draw forth, so a peace succeeding might coffer up. And because he knew his people were hot upon the business, he chose rather to seem to be deceived and lulled asleep by the French than to be backward in himself, considering his subjects were not so fully capable of the reasons of state that made him hold back.

Wherefore, to all these purposes he saw no other expedient than to set and keep on foot a continual treaty of peace, laying it down and taking it up again as the occurrence required. Besides, he had in consideration the point of honour, in bearing the blessed person of a pacificator. He thought likewise to make use of the envy that the French King met with by occasion of this war of Brittany, in strengthening himself with new alliances, as namely that of Ferdinando of Spain, with whom he had ever a consent (even in nature and customs), and likewise with Maximilian, who was particularly interested.[59] So that in substance he promised himself money, honour, friends, and peace in the end. But those things were too fine to be fortunate, and succeed in all parts, for that great affairs are commonly too rough and stubborn to be wrought upon by the finer edges or points of wit. The King was likewise deceived in his two main grounds. For although he had reason to conceive that the council of France would be wary to put the King into a war against the heir apparent of France, yet he did not consider that Charles was not guided by any of the principal of the blood or nobility, but by mean men, who would make it their masterpiece of credit and favour to give venturous counsels that no great or wise man dared or would. And for Maximilian, he was thought then a greater matter than he was, his unstable and necessitous courses being not then known.

After consultation with the ambassadors, who brought him no other news than he expected before (though he would not seem to know it till then), he presently summoned his parliament, and in open parliament propounded the cause of Brittany to both houses by his chancellor, Morton, Archbishop of Canterbury, who spoke to this effect.

'My lords and masters, the King's grace, our sovereign lord, has commanded me to declare unto you the causes that have moved him at this time to summon this his parliament, which I shall do in few words; craving pardon of his grace and you all, if I perform it not as I would.

'His grace does first of all let you know that he retains in thankful memory the love and loyalty showed to him by you at your last meeting, in establishment of his royalty, freeing and discharging of his partakers, and confiscation of his traitors and rebels; more than which could not come from subjects to their sovereign in one action. This he takes so well at your hands, as he has made it a resolution to himself to communicate with so loving and well-approved subjects in all affairs that are of public nature at home or abroad.

'Two therefore are the causes of your present assembling: the one foreign business; the other matters of government at home.

'The French King (as no doubt you have heard) makes at this present hot war upon the Duke of Brittany. His army is now before Nantes, and holds it straitly besieged, being the principal city, if not in ceremony and pre-eminence yet in strength and wealth of that duchy:

you may guess at his hopes, by his attempting of the hardest part of the war first. The cause of this war he knows best. He alleges the entertaining and succouring of the Duke of Orleans and some other French lords, whom the King takes for his enemies. Others divine of other matters. Both parts have by their ambassadors divers times prayed the King's aids; the French King, aids or neutrality; the Bretons, aids simply; for so their case requires. The King, as a Christian prince and blessed son of the holy church, has offered himself as a mediator to treat a peace between them. The French King yielded to treat, but will not stay the prosecution of the war. The Bretons, that desire peace most, hearken to it least; not upon confidence or stiffness but upon distrust of true meaning, seeing the war goes on. So as the King, after as much pains and care to effect a peace as ever he took in any business, not being able to remove the prosecution on the one side, nor the distrust on the other caused by that prosecution, has let fall the treaty, not repenting of it, but despairing of it now as not likely to succeed. Therefore by this narrative you now understand the state of the question, whereupon the King prays your advice, which is no other, but whether he shall enter into an auxiliary and defensive war for the Bretons against France?

'And the better to open your understandings in this affair, the King has commanded me to say somewhat to you from him of the persons that do intervene in this business; and somewhat of the consequence thereof, as it has relation to this kingdom; and somewhat of the example of it in general; making nevertheless no conclusion or judgement of any point, until his grace has received faithful and politic advices.

'First for the King our sovereign himself, who is the principal person you are to eye in this business; his grace does profess that he truly and constantly desires to reign in peace, but his grace says he will neither buy peace with dishonour, nor take it up at interest of danger to ensue, but shall think it a good change, if it please God to change the inward troubles and seditions wherewith he has been hitherto exercised into an honourable foreign war.

'And for the other two persons in this action, the French King and the Duke of Brittany, his grace does declare unto you that they be the men unto whom he is of all other friends and allies most bounden: the one having held over him his hand of protection from the tyrant; the other having reached forth unto him his hand of help for the recovery of his kingdom; so that his affection toward them in his natural person is upon equal terms. And whereas you may have heard that his grace was enforced to fly out of Brittany into France, for doubts of being betrayed, his grace would not in any sort have that reflect upon the Duke of Brittany in defacement of his former benefits, for that he is thoroughly informed that it was but the practice of some corrupt persons about him, during the time of his sickness, altogether without his consent or privity. But howsoever these things do interest his grace in his particular, yet he knows well that the higher bond that ties him to procure by all means the safety and welfare of his loving subjects, does disinterest him of these obligations of gratitude, otherwise than thus, that if his grace be forced to make a war he do it without passion or ambition.

'For the consequence of this action towards this kingdom, it is much as the French King's intention is. For if it be no more but to range his subjects to reason who bear themselves stout upon the strength of the Duke of Brittany, it is nothing to us. But if it be in the French King's purpose – or if it should not be in his purpose, yet if it shall follow all one as if it were sought – that the French King shall make a province of Brittany and join it to the crown of France, then it is worthy the consideration how this may import England, as well in the increasement of the greatness of France by the addition of such a country that stretches his boughs unto our seas, as in depriving this nation and leaving it naked of so firm and assured confederates as the Bretons have always been. For then it will come to pass that, whereas not long since this realm was mighty upon the continent, first in territory and after in alliance, in respect of Burgundy and Brittany, which were confederates indeed but dependent confederates, now the one being already cast partly into the greatness of France and partly into that of Austria,[60] the other is like wholly to be cast into the greatness of France; and this island shall remain confined in effect within the salt waters, and girt about with the coast countries of two mighty monarchs.

'For the example, it rests likewise upon the same question, upon the French King's intent. For if Brittany be carried and swallowed up by

France, as the world abroad (apt to impute and construe the actions of princes to ambition) conceive it will, then it is an example very dangerous and universal, that the lesser neighbour estate should be devoured of the greater. For this may be the case of Scotland towards England; of Portugal towards Spain; of the smaller estates of Italy towards the greater; and so of Germany; or as if some of you of the commons might not live and dwell safely besides some of these great lords. And the bringing in of this example will be chiefly laid to the King's charge,[61] as to him that was most interested and most able to forbid it. But then on the other side, there is so fair a pretext on the French King's part (and yet pretext is never wanting to power), in regard the danger imminent to his own estate is such as may make this enterprise seem rather a work of necessity than of ambition, as does in reason correct the danger of the example, for that the example of that which is done in a man's own defence cannot be dangerous, because it is in another's power to avoid it. But in all this business, the King remits himself to your grave and mature advice, whereupon he purposes to rely.'

This was the effect of the Lord Chancellor's speech touching the cause of Brittany, for the King had commanded him to carry it so as to affect the parliament towards the business, but without engaging the King in any express declaration.

The Chancellor went on:

'For that which may concern the government at home, the King has commanded me to say unto you that he thinks there was never any king (for the small time that he has reigned) had greater and juster cause of the two contrary passions of joy and sorrow than his grace has: joy, in respect of the rare and visible favours of Almighty God in girting the imperial sword upon his side, and assisting the same his sword against all his enemies, and likewise in blessing him with so many good and loving servants and subjects, which have never failed to give him faithful counsel, ready obedience, and courageous defence; sorrow, for that it has not pleased God to suffer him to sheath his sword (as he greatly desired, otherwise than for administration of justice), but that he has been forced to draw it so oft to cut off traitorous and disloyal subjects, whom it seems God has left (a few amongst many good) as the

Canaanites amongst the people of Israel, to be thorns in their sides, to tempt and try them, though the end has been always (God's name be blessed therefore) that the destruction has fallen upon their own heads.

'Wherefore his grace says that he sees that it is not the blood spilled in the field that will save the blood in the city, nor the marshal's sword that will set this kingdom in perfect peace, but that the true way is to stop the seeds of sedition and rebellion in their beginnings, and for that purpose to devise, confirm, and quicken good and wholesome laws against riots and unlawful assemblies of people and all combinations and confederacies of them by liveries, tokens, and other badges of factious dependence; that the peace of the land may by these ordinances, as by bars of iron, be soundly bound in and strengthened, and all force both in court, country, and private houses be suppressed.

'The care hereof, which so much concerns yourselves, and which the nature of the times does instantly call for, his grace commends to your wisdoms.

'And because it is the King's desire that this peace wherein he hopes to govern and maintain you do not bear only unto you leaves, for you to sit under the shade of them in safety, but also should bear you fruit of riches, wealth, and plenty, therefore his grace prays you to take into consideration matter of trade, as also the manufactures of the kingdom, and to repress the bastard and barren employment of moneys to usury and unlawful exchanges, that they may be (as their natural use is) turned upon commerce and lawful and royal trading, and likewise that our people be set awork in arts and handicrafts, that the realm may subsist more of itself, that idleness be avoided, and the draining out of our treasure for foreign manufactures stopped. But you are not to rest here only, but to provide further that whatsoever merchandise shall be brought in from beyond the seas may be employed upon the commodities of this land, whereby the kingdom's stock of treasure may be sure to be kept from being diminished by any overtrading of the foreigner.

'And lastly, because the King is well assured that you would not have him poor that wishes you rich, he doubts not but that you will have care as well to maintain his revenues of customs and all other natures, as also to supply him with your loving aids, if the case shall so require: the rather for that you know the King is a good husband, and but a steward in effect for the public, and that what comes from you is but as moisture drawn from the earth, which gathers into a cloud and falls back upon the earth again, and you know well how the kingdoms about you grow more and more in greatness, and the times are stirring, and therefore not fit to find the King with an empty purse. More I have not to say to you, and wish that what has been said had been better expressed, but that your wisdoms and good affections will supply. God bless your doings.'

It was no hard matter to dispose and affect the parliament in this business, as well in respect of the emulation between the nations, and the envy at the late growth of the French monarchy, as in regard of the danger to suffer the French to make their approaches upon England by obtaining so goodly a maritime province full of sea towns and havens, that might do mischief to the English either by invasion or by interruption of traffic.

The parliament was also moved with the point of oppression, for although the French seemed to speak reason, yet arguments are ever with multitudes too weak for suspicions. Wherefore they did advise the King roundly to embrace the Bretons' quarrel, and to send them speedy aids, and with much alacrity and forwardness granted to the King a great rate of subsidy[62] in contemplation of these aids. But the King, both to keep a decency towards the French King, to whom he professed himself to be obliged, and indeed, desirous rather to show war than to make it, sent new solemn ambassadors to intimate unto him the decree of his estates, and to iterate his motion that the French would desist from hostility; or if war must follow, to desire him to take it in good part if, at the motion of his people, who were sensible of the cause of the Bretons as their ancient friends and confederates, he did send them succours, with protestation nevertheless that, to save all treaties and laws of friendship, he had limited his forces to proceed in aid of the Bretons but in no wise to war upon the French, otherwise than as they maintained the possession of Brittany. But before this formal ambassage arrived, the party of the Duke had received a great blow, and grew to manifest declination. For near the town of St Aubin in Brittany a battle had been given, where the Bretons were overthrown, and the Duke of

Orleans and the Prince of Orange taken prisoners, there being slain on the Bretons' part 6,000 men, and amongst them the Lord Woodville and almost all his soldiers, valiantly fighting. And of the French part, 1,200, with their leader James Galeot, a great commander.

When the news of this battle came over into England, it was time for the King (who now had no subterfuge to continue further treaty, and saw before his eyes that Brittany went so speedily for lost, contrary to his hopes; knowing also that with his people and foreigners both he sustained no small envy and disreputation for his former delays) to despatch with all possible speed his succours into Brittany. Which he did under the conduct of Robert Lord Brook, to the number of 8,000, choice men and well armed, who having a fair wind in few hours landed in Brittany, and joined themselves forthwith to those Breton forces that remained after the defeat, and marched straight on to find the enemy, and encamped fast by them. The French, wisely husbanding the possession of a victory, and well acquainted with the courage of the English, especially when they are fresh, kept themselves within their trenches, being strongly lodged, and resolved not to give battle. But meanwhile, to harass and weary the English, they did upon all advantages set upon them with their light horse, wherein nevertheless they received commonly loss, especially by means of the English archers.

But upon these achievements Francis Duke of Brittany deceased, an accident that the King might easily have foreseen, and ought to have reckoned upon and provided for, but that the point of reputation, when news first came of the battle lost (that somewhat must be done) did overbear the reason of war.

After the Duke's decease the principal persons of Brittany, partly bought, partly through faction, put all things into confusion, so as the English, not finding head or body with whom to join their forces, and being in jealousy of friends as well as in danger of enemies, and the winter begun, returned home five months after their landing. So the battle of St Aubin, the death of the Duke, and the retire of the English succours, were (after some time) the causes of the loss of that duchy, which action some accounted as a blemish of the King's judgement, but most but as the misfortune of his times.

But howsoever the temporary fruit of the parliament in their aid and advice given for Brittany, took not[63] nor prospered not, yet the lasting fruit of parliament, which is good and wholesome laws, did prosper, and does yet continue till this day. For according to the Lord Chancellor's admonition, there were that parliament divers excellent laws ordained, concerning the points which the King recommended.

First, the authority of the Star Chamber,[64] which before subsisted by the ancient common laws of the realm, was confirmed in certain cases by act of parliament. This court is one of the sagest and noblest institutions of this kingdom. For in the distribution of courts of ordinary justice (besides the High Court of parliament), in which distribution the king's bench holds the pleas of the crown; the Common-place, pleas civil; the Exchequer, pleas concerning the King's revenue; and the Chancery, the Pretorian power[65] for mitigating the rigour of law, in case of extremity, by the conscience of a good man; there was nevertheless always reserved a high and pre-eminent power to the King's council in causes that might in example or consequence concern the state of the commonwealth, which if they were criminal, the council used to sit in the chamber called the Star Chamber; if civil, in the white chamber or Whitehall. And as the Chancery had the Pretorian power for equity, so the Star Chamber had the Censorian power[66] for offences under the degree of capital.[67] This court of Star Chamber is compounded of good elements, for it consists of four kinds of persons: councillors, peers, prelates, and chief judges; it discerns also principally of four kinds of causes: forces,[68] frauds, crimes various of stellionate, and the inchoations or middle acts towards crimes capital or heinous not actually committed or perpetrated. But that which was principally aimed at by this act was force, and the two chief supports of force, combination of multitudes, and maintenance or headship of great persons.

From the general peace of the country the King's care went on to the peace of the King's house, and the security of his great officers and councillors. But this law was somewhat of a strange composition and temper: that if any of the King's servants under the degree of a lord, do conspire the death of any of the King's council, or lord of the realm, it is made capital. This law was thought to be procured by the Lord Chancellor, who being a stern and haughty man, and finding he had some mortal enemies in court, provided for his own safety, drowning the envy of it in a general law by communicating the privilege with all other counsellors and peers, and yet not daring to extend it further than to the King's servants in check-roll,[69] lest it should have been too harsh to the gentlemen and other commons of the kingdom, who might have thought their ancient liberty and the clemency of the laws of England invaded, 'if the will in any case of felony should be made the deed'.[70] And yet the reason that the act yields (that is to say, that he that conspires the death of counsellors may be thought indirectly and by a mean to conspire the death of the King himself) is indifferent to all subjects as well as to servants in court. But it seems this sufficed to serve the Lord Chancellor's turn at this time; but yet he lived to need a general law, for that he grew afterwards as odious to the country as he was then to the court.

From the peace of the King's house the King's care extended to the peace of private houses and families, for there was an excellent moral law moulded thus: the taking and carrying away of women forcibly and against their will (except female wards and bond-women) was made capital: the parliament wisely and justly conceiving that the obtaining of women by force into possession (howsoever afterwards assent might follow by allurements) was but a rape drawn forth in length, because the first force drew on all the rest.

There was made also another law for peace in general, and repressing of murders and manslaughters, and was in amendment of the common laws of the realm, being this: that whereas by common law the King's suit, in case of homicide, did expect the year and the day,[71] allowed to the party's suit by way of appeal, and that it was found by experience that the party was many times compounded with, and many times wearied with the suit, so that in the end such suit was let fall, and by that time the matter was in a manner forgotten, and thereby prosecution at the King's suit by indictment (which is ever best *flagrante crimine*) neglected; it was ordained that the suit by indictment might be taken as well at any time within the year and the day as after, not prejudicing nevertheless the party's suit.

The King began also then, as well in wisdom as in justice, to pare a little the privilege of clergy,[72] ordaining that clerks convict should be burned in the hand – both because they might taste of some corporal punishment, and that they might carry a brand of infamy. But for this good act's sake, the King himself was after branded by Perkin's proclamation for an execrable breaker of the rites of holy church.

Another law was made for the better peace of the country, by which law the King's officers and farmers were to forfeit their places and holds, in case of unlawful retainer[73] or partaking in routs and unlawful assemblies.

These were the laws that were made for repressing of force that those times did chiefly require, and were so prudently framed as they are found fit for all succeeding times, and so continue to this day.

There were also made good and politic laws that parliament against usury, which is the bastard use of money, and against unlawful chievances and exchanges, which is bastard usury, and also for the security of the King's customs, and for the employment of the procedures of foreign commodities, brought in by merchants strangers, upon the native commodities of the realm, together with some other laws of less importance.

But howsoever the laws made in that parliament did bear good and wholesome fruit, yet the subsidy granted at the same time bore a fruit that proved harsh and bitter. All was inned at last into the King's barn, but it was after a storm. For when the commissioners entered into the taxation of the subsidy in Yorkshire and the bishopric of Durham, the people upon a sudden grew into great mutiny, and said openly that they had endured of late years a thousand miseries, and neither could nor would pay the subsidy. This no doubt proceeded not simply of any present necessity, but much by reason of the old humour of those countries, where the memory of King Richard was so strong, that it lay like lees in the bottom of men's hearts, and if the vessel was but stirred it would come up, and no doubt it was partly also by the instigation of some factious malcontents that bore principal stroke[74] amongst them.

Hereupon the commissioners, being somewhat astonished, deferred the matter unto the Earl of Northumberland, who was the principal man of authority in those parts. The Earl forthwith wrote unto the court, signifying to the King plainly enough in what flame he found the people of those countries, and praying the King's direction. The King wrote back peremptorily that he would not have one penny abated of that which had been granted to him by parliament, both because it might encourage other countries to pray the like release or mitigation, and chiefly because he would never endure that the base multitude should frustrate the authority of the parliament, wherein their votes and consents were concluded. Upon this despatch from court, the Earl assembled the principal justices and freeholders of the country, and speaking to them in the imperious language wherein the King had written him, which needed not (save that a harsh business was unfortunately fallen into the hands of a harsh man), did not only irritate the people, but make them conceive by the stoutness and haughtiness of delivery of the King's errand, that himself[75] was the author or principal persuader of that counsel, whereupon the meaner sort routed together, and suddenly assailing the Earl in his house, slew him and divers of his servants, and rested not there, but creating for their leader Sir John Egremond, a factious person, and one that had of a long time borne an ill talent towards the King, and being animated also by a base fellow, called John a Chamber, a very *boutefeu*, who bore much sway amongst the vulgar and populace, entered into open rebellion, and gave out in flat terms that they would go against King Henry and fight with him for the maintenance of their liberties.

When the King was advertised of this new insurrection (being almost a fever that took him every year), after his manner little troubled therewith, he sent Thomas Earl of Surrey (whom he had a little before not only released out of the Tower and pardoned, but also received to especial favour) with a competent power against the rebels, who fought with the principal band of them and defeated them, and took alive John a Chamber their firebrand. As for Sir John Egremond, he fled into Flanders to the Lady Margaret Burgundy, whose palace was the sanctuary and receptacle of traitors against the King. John a Chamber was executed at York in great state, for he was hanged upon a gibbet raised a stage higher in the midst of a square gallows, as a traitor paramount, and a number of his men that were his chief complices were hanged upon the lower story round about him; and the rest were generally pardoned. Neither did the King himself omit his custom to be first or second in all his warlike exploits, making good his word that was usual with him when he heard of rebels, 'that he desired but to see them'. For immediately after he had sent down the Earl of Surrey, he marched towards them himself in person. And although in his journey he heard news of the victory, yet he went on as far as York to pacify and settle those countries, and that done, returned to London, leaving the Earl of Surrey for his lieutenant in the northern parts, and Sir Richard Tunstall for his principal commissioner to levy the subsidy, whereof he did not remit a denier.[76]

About the same time that the King lost so good a servant as the Earl of Northumberland, he lost likewise a faithful friend and ally in James the Third, King of Scotland, by a miserable disaster. For this unfortunate prince, after a long smother of discontent and hatred of many of his nobility and people, breaking forth at times into seditions and alterations of court, was at last distressed by them, having taken arms and surprised the person of Prince James his son (partly by force, partly by threats that they would otherwise deliver up the kingdom to the King of England) to shadow their rebellion, and to be the titular and painted head of those arms. Whereupon the King (finding himself too weak) sought unto King Henry, as also unto the Pope and the King of France, to compose those troubles between him and his subjects. The kings accordingly interposed their mediations in a round and princely manner, not only by way of request and persuasion, but also by way of protestation and menace, declaring that they thought it to be the common cause of all kings, if subjects should be suffered to give laws unto their sovereign, and that they would accordingly resent and revenge it. But the rebels, that had shaken off the greater yoke of obedience, had likewise cast away the lesser tie of respect, and fury prevailing above fear, made answer, that there was no talking of peace except their king would resign his crown. Whereupon (treaty of accord taking no place) it came to a battle at Bannocksbourn by Stirling. In which battle the King[77] transported with wrath and just indignation, inconsiderately fighting and precipitating the charge before his whole numbers came up to him, was, notwithstanding the contrary express and strait commandment of the Prince his son, slain in the pursuit, being fled to a mill situate in the field where the battle was fought.

As for the Pope's ambassy, which was sent by[78] Adrian de Castello, an Italian legate (and perhaps as those times were might have prevailed more), it came too late for the ambassy, but not for ambassador. For passing through England and being honourably entertained and received of King Henry (who ever applied himself with much respect to the see of Rome), he fell into great grace with the King, and great familiarity and friendship with Morton the Chancellor. Insomuch as the King, taking a liking to him and finding him to his mind, preferred him to the bishopric of Hereford, and afterwards to that of Bath and Wells, and employed him in many of his affairs of state that had relation to Rome. He was a man of great learning, wisdom, and dexterity in business of state and having not long after ascended to the degree of cardinal, paid the King large tribute of his gratitude in diligent and judicious advertisement of the occurrents of Italy. Nevertheless, in the end of his time he was partaker of the conspiracy that Cardinal Alphonso Petrucci and some other cardinals had plotted against the life of Pope Leo. And this offence, in itself so heinous, was yet in him aggravated by the motive thereof, which was not malice or discontent, but an aspiring mind to the papacy. And in this he of impiety there wanted not an intermixture of levity and folly, for that (as was generally believed) he was animated to expect the papacy by a fatal mockery, the prediction of a soothsayer, which was, 'That one should succeed Pope Leo, whose name should be Adrian, an aged man of mean birth and of great learning and wisdom'; by which character and figure he took himself to be described, though it were fulfilled of Adrian the Fleming, son to a Dutch brewer, Cardinal of Tortosa, and preceptor unto Charles the Fifth, the same that, not changing his christen-name, was afterwards called Adrian the Sixth.

But these things happened in the year following, which was the fifth of this king. But in the end of the fourth year the King had called again his parliament, not as it seems for any particular occasion of state, but the former parliament being ended somewhat suddenly (in regard of the preparation for Brittany), the King thought he had not remunerated his people sufficiently with good laws (which evermore was his retribution for treasure), and finding by the insurrection in the north, there was discontentment abroad in respect of the subsidy, he thought it good for to give his subjects yet further contentment and comfort in that kind. Certainly his times for good commonwealths' laws did excel, so as he may justly be celebrated for the best lawgiver to this nation after King Edward the First. For his laws (whoso marks them well) are deep and not vulgar; not made upon the spur of a particular occasion for the present, but out of providence of the future; to make the estate of his people still more and more happy, after the manner of the legislators in ancient and heroical times.

First therefore he made a law suitable to his own acts and times. For as himself had in his person and marriage made a final concord in the great suit and title for the crown, so by this law he settled the like peace and quiet in the private possessions of the subjects, ordaining, that fines[79] thenceforth should be final to conclude all strangers' rights, and that upon fines levied, and solemnly proclaimed, the subject should have his time of watch for five years after his title accrued, which if he forepassed, his right should be bound for ever after, with some exception nevertheless of minors, married women, and such incompetent persons. This statute did in effect but restore an ancient statute of the realm, which was itself also made but in affirmance of the common law. The alteration had been by a statute commonly called the statute of *non-claim*, made in the time of Edward the Third. And surely this law was a kind of prognostic of the good peace that since his time has (for the most part) continued in this kingdom until this day. For statutes of *non-claim* are fit for times of war, when men's heads are troubled, that they cannot intend their estate, but statutes that quiet possessions are fittest for times of peace, to extinguish suits and contentions, which is one of the banes of peace.

Another statute was made, of singular policy, for the population apparently, and (if it be thoroughly considered) for the soldiery and military forces of the realm. Enclosures at that time began to be more frequent, whereby arable land (which could not be manured without people and families) was turned into pasture, which was easily rid by a few herdsmen, and tenances for years, lives, and at will (whereupon much of the yeomanry lived), were turned into demesnes. This bred a decay of people, and by consequence a decay of towns, churches, tithes, and the like. The King likewise knew full well, and in no wise forgot, that there ensued withal upon this a decay and diminution of subsidies and taxes, for the more gentlemen, ever the lower books of subsidies. In remedying of this inconvenience the King's wisdom was admirable, and the parliament's at that time. Enclosures they would not forbid, for that had been to forbid the improvement of the patrimony of the kingdom, nor tillage they would not compel, for that was to strive with nature and utility. But they took a course to take away depopulating enclosures and depopulating pasturage and yet not that by name, or by any imperious express prohibition, but by consequence. The ordinance was, that all houses of husbandry, that were used with twenty acres of ground and upwards, should be maintained and kept up forever, together with a competent proportion of land to be used and occupied with them, and in no wise to be severed from them (as by another statute, made afterwards in his successor's time, was more fully declared); this upon forfeitures to be taken, not by way of popular action, but by seizure of the land itself by the King and lords of the fee, as to half the profits, till the houses and lands were restored.

By this means the houses being kept up did of necessity enforce a dweller, and the proportion of land for occupation being kept up, did of necessity enforce that dweller not to be a beggar or cottager, but a man of some substance, that might keep hinds and servants, and set the plough on going. This did wonderfully concern the might and mannerhood of the kingdom, to have farms as it were of a standard sufficient to maintain an able body out of penury, and did in effect amortise a great part of the lands of the kingdom unto the hold and occupation of the yeomanry or middle people, of a condition between gentlemen and cottagers or peasants.

Now how much this did advance the military power of the kingdom is apparent by the true principles of war and the examples of other kingdoms. For it has been held by the general opinion of men of best judgement in the wars (howsoever some few have varied, and that it may receive some distinction of case[80]) that the principal strength of an army consists in the infantry or foot. And to make good infantry, it requires men bred not in a servile or indigent fashion, but in some free and plentiful manner. Therefore if a state run most to noblemen and gentlemen, and that the husbandmen and ploughmen be but as their workfolks or labourers, or else mere cottagers (which are but housed beggars), you may have a good cavalry, but never good stable bands of foot, like to coppice woods, that if you leave in them staddles too thick, they will run to bushes and briars, and have little clean underwood. And this is to be seen in France and Italy (and some other parts abroad), where in effect all is noblesse or peasantry (I speak of people out of towns), and no middle people, and therefore no good forces of foot insomuch as they are enforced to employ mercenary bands of Switzers (and the like) for their battalions of foot. Whereby also it comes to pass that those nations have much people and few soldiers. Whereas the King saw that contrariwise it would follow that England, though much less in territory, yet should have infinitely more soldiers of their native forces than those other nations have. Thus did the King secretly sow Hydra's teeth;[81] whereupon (according to the poets' fiction) should rise up armed men for the service of this kingdom.

The King also (having care to make his realm potent as well by sea as by land), for the better maintenance of the navy, ordained that wines and woads from the parts of Gascony and Languedoc, should not be brought but in English bottoms, bowing the ancient policy of this estate from consideration of plenty to consideration of power, for that almost all the ancient statutes invite (by all means) merchants strangers to bring in all sorts of commodities, having for end cheapness, and not looking to the point of state concerning the naval power.

The King also made a statute in that parliament monitory and minatory towards justices of peace, that they should duly execute their office, inviting complaints against them, first to their fellow justices, then to the justices of assize, then to the King or Chancellor, and that a proclamation that he had published of that tenor should be read in open session four times a year, to keep them awake. Meaning also to have his laws executed, and thereby to reap either obedience or forfeitures (wherein towards his later times he did decline too much to the left hand[82]), he did ordain remedy against the practice that was grown in use, to stop and damp informations upon penal laws by procuring informations by collusion to be put in by the confederates of the delinquents, to be faintly prosecuted and let fall at pleasure, and pleading them in bar of the informations which were prosecuted with effect.[83]

He made also laws for the correction of the mint, and counterfeiting of foreign coin current. And that no payment in gold should be made to any merchant stranger, the better to keep treasure within the realm, for that gold was the metal that lay in least room.

He made also statutes for the maintenance of drapery and the keeping of wools within the realm, and not only so, but for stinting and limiting the prices of cloth: one for the finer, and another for the coarser sort. Which I note, both because it was a rare thing to set prices by statute, especially upon our home commodities, and because of the wise model of this act: not prescribing prices, but stinting them not to exceed a rate, that the clothier might drape accordingly as he might afford.

Divers other good statutes were made that parliament, but these were the principal. And here I do desire those into whose hand this work shall fall, that they do take in good part my long insisting upon the laws that were made in this King's reign, whereof I have these reasons, both because it was the pre-eminent virtue and merit of this King, to whose memory I do honour, and because it has some correspondence to my person, but chiefly because in my judgement it is some defect even in the best writers of history, that they do not often enough summarily deliver and set down the most memorable laws that passed in the times whereof they write, being indeed the principal acts of peace. For though they may be had in original books of law themselves, yet that informs not the judgement of kings and counsellors and persons of estate so well as to see them described and entered in the table and portrait of the times.

About the same time the King had a loan from the city of 4,000 pounds, which was double to that they lent before, and was duly and orderly paid back at the day, as the former likewise had been, the King ever choosing rather to borrow too soon than to pay too late, and so keeping up his credit.

Neither had the King yet cast off his cares and hopes touching Brittany, but thought to master the occasion by policy, though his arms had been unfortunate, and to bereave the French King of the fruit of his victory. The sum of his design was to encourage Maximilian to go on with his suit for the marriage of Anne, the heir of Brittany, and to aid him to the consummation thereof. But the affairs of Maximilian were at that time in great trouble and combustion, by a rebellion of his subjects in Flanders, especially those of Bruges and Ghent, whereof the town of Bruges (at such time as Maximilian was there in person) had suddenly armed in tumult and slain some of his principal officers, and taken himself prisoner and held him in durance till they had enforced him and some of his counsellors to take a solemn oath to pardon all their offences, and never to question and revenge the same in time to come. Nevertheless Frederick the Emperor would not suffer this reproach and indignity offered to his son to pass, but made sharp war upon Flanders to reclaim and chastise the rebels. But the Lord Ravenstein, a principal person about Maximilian and one that had taken the oath of abolition[84] with his master, pretending the religion thereof,[85] but indeed upon private ambition (and as it was thought instigated and corrupted from France), forsook the Emperor and Maximilian his lord, and made himself a head of the popular party, and seized upon the towns of Ypres and Sluice with both the castles, and forthwith sent to the Lord Cordes, governor of Picardy under the French King, to desire aid, and to move him that he on the behalf of the French King would be protector of the united towns, and by force of arms reduce the rest. The Lord Cordes was ready to embrace the occasion, which was partly of his own setting, and sent forthwith greater forces than it had been possible for him to raise on the sudden if he had not looked for such a summons before, in aid of the Lord Ravenstein and the Flemings, with instructions to invest the towns between France and Bruges. The French forces besieged a little town called Dixmude, where part of the Flemish forces joined with them.

While they lay at this siege the King of England, upon pretence of the safety of the English pale about Calais (but in truth being loath that Maximilian should become contemptible and thereby be shaken off by the states of Brittany about his marriage), sent over the Lord Morley with a thousand men unto the Lord Daubeney, then deputy of Calais, with secret instructions to aid Maximilian and to raise the siege of Dixmude. The Lord Daubeney (giving out that all was for the strengthening of the English marches) drew out of the garrisons of Calais, Hammes, and Guines, to the number of a thousand men more, so that with the fresh succours that came under the conduct of the Lord Morley, they made up to the number of 2,000 or better. Which forces, joining with some companies of Almains, put themselves into Dixmude, not perceived by the enemies, and passing through the town (with some reinforcement from the forces that were in the town) assailed the enemies' camp, negligently guarded as being out of fear, where there was a bloody fight, in which the English and their partakers obtained the victory, and slew to the number of 8,000 men, with the loss on the English part of a hundred or thereabouts, amongst whom was the Lord Morley. They took also their great ordnance, with much rich spoils, which they carried to Newport, whence the Lord Daubeney returned to Calais, leaving the hurt men and some other voluntaries in Newport.

But the Lord Cordes being at Ypres with a great power of men, thinking to recover the loss and disgrace of the fight at Dixmude, came presently on and sat down before Newport and besieged it. And after some days' siege he resolved to try the fortune of an assault, which he did one day, and succeeded therein so far that he had taken the principal tower and fort in that city, and planted upon it the French banner, whence nevertheless they were presently beaten forth by the English, by the help of some fresh succours of archers, arriving by good fortune (at the instant) in the haven of Newport. Whereupon the Lord Cordes, discouraged, and measuring the new succours that were small by the success that was great, left his siege. By this means matters grew more exasperate between the two kings of England and France, for that in the war of Flanders the auxiliary forces of French and English were much blooded one against another, which blood rankled the more by the vain words of the Lord Cordes, that declared himself an open enemy of the English, beyond that that appertained to the present service, making it a common byword of his, that he could be content to lie in hell seven years so he might win Calais from the English.

The King having thus upheld the reputation of Maximilian, advised him now to press on his marriage with Brittany to a conclusion, which Maximilian accordingly did, and so far forth prevailed both with the young lady and with the principal persons about her, as the marriage was consummate by proxy with a ceremony at that time in these parts new. For she was not only publicly contracted, but stated as a bride, and solemnly bedded,[86] and after she was laid, there came in Maximilian's ambassador with letters of procuration, and in the presence of sundry noble personages, men and women, put his leg (stripped naked to the knee) between the espousal sheets, to the end that that ceremony might be thought to amount to a consummation and actual knowledge. This done, Maximilian (whose property[87] was to leave things then when they were almost come to perfection, and to end them by imagination, like ill archers, that draw not their arrows up to the head, and who might as easily have bedded the lady himself as to have made a play and disguise of it), thinking now all assured, neglected for a time his further proceeding, and intended his wars.

Meanwhile the French King (consulting with his divines, and finding that this pretended consummation was rather an invention of court than any ways valid by the laws of the church), went more really to work, and by secret instruments and cunning agents – as well matrons about the young lady as counsellors – first sought to remove the point of religion and honour out of the mind of the lady herself, wherein there was a double labour, for Maximilian was not only contracted unto the lady, but Maximilian's daughter was likewise contracted to King Charles: so as the marriage halted upon both feet, and was not clear on either side. But for the contract with King Charles, the exception lay plain and fair, for that Maximilian's daughter was under years of consent, and so not bound by law, but a power of disagreement left to either part. But for the contract made by Maximilian with the lady herself, they were harder driven, having nothing to allege but that it was done without the consent of her sovereign lord King Charles, whose ward and client she was, and he to her in place of a father, and therefore it was void and of no force, for want of such consent. Which defect (they said) though it would not evacuate a marriage after cohabitation and actual consummation, yet it was enough to make void a contract. For as for the pretended consummation, they made sport with it and said that it was an argument that Maximilian was a widower and a cold wooer, that could content himself to be a bridegroom by deputy, and would not make a little journey to put all out of question. So that the young lady, wrought upon by these reasons finely instilled by such as the French King (who spared for no rewards or promises) had made on his side, and allured likewise by the present glory and greatness of King Charles (being also a young king and a bachelor), and loath to make her country the seat of a long and miserable war, secretly yielded to accept of King Charles.

But during this secret treaty with the lady, the better to save it from blasts of opposition and interruption, King Charles, resorting to his wonted arts, and thinking to carry the marriage as he had carried the wars by entertaining the King of England in vain belief, sent a solemn ambassage by Francis Lord of Luxemburg, Charles Marignian, and Robert Gagvien, general of the order of the *bons-hommes* of the Trinity,[88] to treat a peace and league with the King, accoupling it with an article in the nature of a request, that the French King might with the King's good will (according unto his right of seigniory and tutelage) dispose of the marriage of the young Duchess of Brittany as he should think good, offering by judicial proceeding to make void the marriage of Maximilian by proxy. Also all this while, the better to amuse the world, he did continue in his court and custody the daughter of Maximilian, who formerly had been sent unto him to be bred and educated in France, not dismissing or renvoying her but contrariwise professing and giving out strongly that he meant to proceed with that match, and that for the Duchess of Brittany, he desired only to present his right of seigniory, and to give her in marriage to some such ally as might depend upon him.

When the three commissioners came to the court of England they delivered their ambassage unto the King, who remitted them to his council, where some days after they had audience, and made their proposition by the Prior of the Trinity (who though he were third in place, yet was held the best speaker of them) to this effect:

'My lords, the King our master, the greatest and mightiest king that reigned in France since Charles the great[89] whose name he bears, has nevertheless thought it no disparagement to his greatness at this time to propound a peace, yea and to pray a peace, with the King of England. For which purpose he has sent us his commissioners, instructed and enabled with full and ample power to treat and conclude, giving us further in charge to open in some other business the secrets of his own intentions. These be indeed the precious love tokens between great kings, to communicate one with another the true state of their affairs, and to pass by nice points of honour, which ought not to give law unto affection. This I do assure your lordships, it is not possible for you to imagine the true and cordial love that the King our master bears to your sovereign, except you were near him as we are. He uses his name with so great respect, he remembers their first acquaintance at Paris with so great contentment, nay he never speaks of him but that presently he falls into discourse of the miseries of great kings, in that they cannot converse with their equals, but with their servants. This affection to your king's person and virtues God has put into the heart of our master, no doubt for the good of Christendom, and for purposes yet unknown to us all; for other root it cannot have, since it was the same to the Earl of Richmond that it is now to the King of England. This is therefore the first motive that makes our king to desire peace and league with your sovereign, good affection, and somewhat that he finds in his own heart. This affection is also armed with reason of estate. For our king does in all candour and frankness of dealing open himself unto you, that having an honourable, yea and holy purpose, to make a voyage and war in remote parts, he considers that it will be of no small effect in point of reputation to his enterprise, if it be known abroad that he is in good peace with all his neighbour princes, and specially with the King of England, whom for good causes he esteems most.

'But now, my lords, give me leave to use a few words to remove all scruples and misunderstandings between your sovereign and ours concerning some late actions, which if they be not cleared, may perhaps hinder this peace, to the end that for matters past neither king may conceive unkindness of other, nor think the other conceives unkindness of him. The late actions are two: that of Brittany, and that of Flanders. In both which it is true that the subjects' swords of both kings have encountered and stricken, and the ways and inclinations also of the two kings in respect of their confederates and allies have severed.

'For that of Brittany: the King your sovereign knows best what has passed. It was a war of necessity on our master's part. And though the motives of it were sharp and piquant as could be, yet did he make that war rather with an olive branch than a laurel branch in his hand, more desiring peace than victory. Besides, from time to time he sent, as it were, blank papers to your king to write the conditions of peace. For though both his honour and safety went upon it, yet he thought neither of them too precious to put into the King of England's hands. Neither does our king on the other side make any unfriendly interpretation of your king's sending of succours to the Duke of Brittany; for the King knows well that many things must be done of kings for satisfaction of their people, and it is not hard to discern what is a king's own. But this matter of Brittany is now by the act of God ended and passed, and, as the King hopes, like the way of a ship in the sea, without leaving any impression in either of the kings' minds, as he is sure for his part it has not done in his.

'For the action of Flanders: as the former of Brittany was a war of necessity, so this was a war of justice, which with a good king is of equal necessity with danger of estate, for else he should leave to be a king. The subjects of Burgundy are subjects in chief to the crown of France, and their duke the homager and vassal of France. They had wont to be good subjects, howsoever Maximilian has of late distempered them. They fled to the King for justice and deliverance from oppression. Justice he could not deny; purchase he did not seek. This was good for Maximilian if he could have seen it in people mutined, to arrest fury and prevent despair. My lords, it may be this I have said is needless, save that the King our master is tender in any thing that may but glance upon the friendship of England. The amity between the two kings no doubt stands entire and inviolate. And that their subjects' swords have clashed, it is nothing unto the public peace of the crowns, it being a thing very usual in auxiliary forces of the best and straitest confederates to meet and draw blood in the field. Nay many times there be aids of the same nation on both sides, and yet it is not for all that a kingdom divided in itself.

'It rests my lords that I impart unto you a matter that I know your lordships all will much rejoice to hear, as that which imports the Christian commonweal more than any action that has happened of long time. The King our master has a purpose and determination to make war upon the kingdom of Naples, being now in the possession of a bastard slip of Aragon, but appertaining unto his majesty by clear and undoubted right,[90] which if he should not by just arms seek to recover, he could neither acquit his honour nor answer it to his people. But his noble and Christian thoughts rest not here, for his resolution and hope is to make the reconquest of Naples but as a bridge to transport his forces into Grecia, and not to spare blood or treasure (if it were to the impawning his crown and dispeopling of France) till either he has overthrown the empire of the Ottomans, or taken it in his way to paradise. The King knows well that this is a design that could not arise in the mind of any king that did not steadfastly look up unto God, whose quarrel this is, and from whom comes both the will and the deed. But yet it is agreeable to the person that he bears (though unworthy) of the Thrice Christian King, and the eldest son of the church, whereunto he is also invited by the example (in more ancient time) of King Henry the Fourth of England (the first renowned King of the house of Lancaster; ancestor though not progenitor to your King), who had a purpose towards the end of his time (as you know better) to make an expedition into the Holy Land, and by the example also (present before his eyes) of that honourable and religious war that the King of Spain now makes and has almost brought to perfection, for the recovery of the realm of Granada from the Moors. And although this enterprise may seem vast and unmeasured, for the King to attempt that by his own forces wherein (heretofore) a conjunction of most of the Christian princes has found work enough; yet his Majesty wisely considers that sometimes smaller forces being united under one command are more effectual in proof, though not so promising in opinion and fame, than much greater forces variously compounded by associations and leagues, which commonly in a short time after their beginnings turn to dissociations and divisions. But, my lords, that which is as a voice from heaven that calls the King to this enterprise, is a rent at this time in the house of the Ottomans. I do not say but there has been brother against brother in that house before, but never that had refuge to the arms of the Christians as now has Gemes (brother under Bajazet that reigns), the far braver man of the two, the other being between a monk and a philosopher, and better read in the Koran and Averroes[91] than able to wield the sceptre of so warlike an empire. This therefore is the King our master's memorable and heroical resolution for a holy war. And because he carries in this the person of a Christian soldier as well as of a great temporal monarch, he begins with humility and is content for this cause to beg peace at the hands of other Christian kings.

'There remains only rather a civil request than any essential part of our negotiation, which the King makes to the King your sovereign. The King (as all the world knows) is lord in chief of the duchy of Brittany. The marriage of the heir belongs to him as guardian. This is a private patrimonial right, and no business of estate. Yet nevertheless (to run a fair course with your king, whom he desires to make another himself, and to be one and the same thing with him), his request is, that with the King's favour and consent he may dispose of her marriage as he thinks good, and make void the intruded and pretended marriage of Maximilian, according to justice.

'This, my lords, is all that I have to say, desiring your pardon for my weakness in the delivery.'

Thus did the French ambassadors, with great show of their king's affection and many sugared words, seek to addulce all matters between the two kings, having two things for their ends: the one, to keep the King quiet till the marriage of Brittany was past and this was but a summer fruit, which they thought was almost ripe, and would be soon gathered. The other was more lasting, and that was to put him into such a temper as he might be no disturbance or impediment to the voyage for Italy.

The lords of the council were silent, and said only that they knew the ambassadors would look for no answer till they had reported to the King. And so they rose from council.

The King could not well tell what to think of the marriage of Brittany. He saw plainly the ambition of the French King was to impatronise himself of the duchy, but he wondered he would bring into his house a litigious marriage, especially considering who was his successor.[92] But weighing one thing with another, he gave Brittany for lost, but resolved to make his profit of this business of Brittany as a quarrel for war, and of that of Naples as a wrench and mean for peace, being well advertised how strongly the King was bent upon that action. Having therefore conferred divers times with his council, and keeping himself somewhat close, he gave a direction to the Chancellor for a formal answer to the ambassadors, and that he did in the presence of his council. And after, calling the Chancellor to him apart, bade him speak in such language as was fit for a treaty that was to end in a breach, and gave him also a special caveat, that he should not use any words to discourage the voyage of Italy. Soon after, the ambassadors were sent for to the council, and the Lord Chancellor spoke to them in this sort:

'My lords ambassadors, I shall make answer, by the King's commandment, unto the eloquent declaration of you my lord Prior, in brief and plain manner. The King forgets not his former love and acquaintance with the King your master. But of this there needs no repetition, for if it be between them as it was, it is well; if there be any alteration, it is not words will make it up. For the business of Brittany, the King finds it a little strange that the French King makes mention of it as matter of well deserving at his hand. For that deserving was no more but to make him his instrument to surprise one of his best confederates. And for the marriage, the King would not meddle in it, if your master would marry by the book, and not by the sword. For that of Flanders, if the subjects of Burgundy had appealed to your King as their chief lord, at first, by way of supplication, it might have had a show of justice. But it was a new form of process, for subjects to imprison their prince first, and to slay his officers, and then to be complainants. The King says that sure he is, when the French King and himself sent to the subjects of Scotland (that had taken arms against their King), they both spoke in another style, and did in princely manner signify their detestation of popular attentates upon the person or authority of princes. But, my lords ambassadors, the King leaves these two actions thus. That on the one side, he has not received any manner of satisfaction from you concerning them, and on the other, that he does not apprehend them so deeply as in respect of them to refuse to treat of peace, if other things may go hand in hand. As for the war of Naples and the design against the Turk, the King has commanded me expressly to say that he does wish with all his heart to his good brother the French King, that his fortunes may succeed according to his hopes and honourable intentions, and whensoever he shall hear that he is prepared for Grecia – as your master is pleased now to say that he begs a peace of the King, so the King then will beg of him a part in that war.

'But now, my lords ambassadors, I am to propound unto you somewhat on the King's part. The King your master has taught our King what to say and demand. You say (my lord Prior) that your King is resolved to recover his right to Naples, wrongfully detained from him, and that if he should not thus do, he could not acquit his honour, nor answer it to his people. Think, my lords, that the King our master says the same thing over again to you, touching Normandy, Guienne, Anjou; yea, and the kingdom of France[93] itself. I cannot express it better than in your own words. If therefore the French King shall consent that the King our master's title to France (or least tribute for the same) be handled in the treaty, the King is content to go on with the rest, otherwise he refuses to treat.'

The ambassadors, being somewhat abashed with this demand, answered in some heat that they doubted not but that the King their sovereign's sword would be able to maintain his sceptre, and they assured themselves, he neither could nor would yield to any diminution of the crown of France, either in territory or regality. But howsoever, they were too great matters for them to speak of, having no commission. It was replied that the King looked for no other answer from them, but would forthwith send his own ambassadors to the French King. There was a question also asked at the table: whether the French King would agree to have the disposing of the marriage of Brittany, with an exception and exclusion that he should not marry her himself? To which the ambassadors answered, that it was so far out of their King's thoughts as they had received no instructions touching the same.

Thus were the ambassadors dismissed, all save the Prior, and were followed immediately by Thomas Earl of Ormond, and Thomas Goldenston, Prior of Christ-Church in Canterbury, who were presently sent over into France. In the mean space Lionel, Bishop of Concordia, was sent as nuncio from Pope Alexander the Sixth to both kings, to move a peace between them. For Pope Alexander, finding himself pent and locked up by a league and association of the principal states of Italy, that he could not make his way for the advancement of his own house (which he immoderately thirsted after), was desirous to trouble the waters in Italy, that he might fish the better; casting the net not out of St Peter's, but out of Borgia's bark. And doubting lest the fears from

England might stay the French King's voyage into Italy, despatched this bishop to compose all matters between the two kings, if he could: who first repaired to the French King, and finding him well inclined (as he conceived), took on his journey towards England, and found the English ambassadors at Calais on their way towards the French King. After some conference with them, he was in honourable manner transported over into England, where he had audience of the King. But notwithstanding he had a good ominous name to have made a peace, nothing followed. For in the meantime the purpose of the French King to marry the Duchess could be no longer dissembled. Wherefore the English ambassadors (finding how things went) took their leave and returned. And the Prior also was warned from hence, to depart out of England. Who when he turned his back (more like a pedant than an ambassador), dispersed a bitter libel in Latin verse against the King, unto which the King (though he had nothing of a pedant) yet was content to cause an answer to be made in like verse, and that as speaking in his own person, but in a style of scorn and sport.

About this time also was born the King's second son Henry, who afterwards reigned.[94] And soon after followed the solemnisation of the marriage between Charles and Anne, Duchess of Brittany, with whom he received the duchy of Brittany as her dowry, the daughter of Maximilian being a little before sent home. Which when it came to the ears of Maximilian (who would never believe it till it was done, being ever the principal in deceiving himself, though in this the French King did very handsomely second it), and tumbling it over and over in his thoughts, that he should at one blow, with such a double scorn, be defeated both of the marriage of his daughter and his own (upon both which he had fixed high imaginations), he lost all patience; and casting off the respects fit to be continued between great kings, even when their blood is hottest and most risen, fell to bitter invectives against the person and actions of the French King, and (by how much he was the less able to do, talking so much the more) spoke all the injuries he could devise of Charles, saying that he was the most perfidious man upon the earth, and that he had made a marriage compounded between an advoultry and a rape, which was done (he said) by the just judgement of God to the end that, the nullity thereof being apparent to all the world, the race of so unworthy a person might not reign in France. And forthwith he sent ambassadors as well to the King of England as to the King of Spain, to incite them to war and to treat a league offensive against France, promising to concur with great forces of his own.

Hereupon the King of England (going nevertheless his own way) called a parliament, it being the seventh year of his reign, and the first day of opening thereof (sitting under his cloth of estate) spoke himself unto his Lords and Commons in this manner.

'My Lords and you the Commons; when I purposed to make a war in Brittany by my lieutenant, I made declaration thereof to you by my Chancellor. But now that I mean to make a war upon France in person, I will declare it to you myself. That war was to defend another man's right, but this is to recover our own; and that ended by accident, but we hope this shall end in victory.

'The French King troubles the Christian world. That which he has is not his own, and yet he seeks more. He has invested himself of Brittany. He maintains the rebels in Flanders, and he threatens Italy. For ourselves, he has proceeded from dissimulation to neglect, and from neglect to contumely. He has assailed our confederates; he denies our tribute; in a word, he seeks war. So did not his father, but sought peace at our hands; and so perhaps will he, when good counsel or time shall make him see as much as his father did.

'Meanwhile, let us make his ambition our advantage, and let us not stand upon a few crowns of tribute or acknowledgement, but by the favour of Almighty God try our right for the crown of France itself, remembering that there has been a French king prisoner[95] in England, and a king of England crowned[96] in France. Our confederates are not diminished. Burgundy is in a mightier hand than ever, and never more provoked. Brittany cannot help us, but it may hurt them. New acquests are more burden than strength. The malcontents of his own kingdom have not been base populace, nor titulary impostors, but of a higher nature. The King of Spain (doubt ye not) will join with us, not knowing where the French King's ambition will stay. Our holy father (the Pope) likes no Tramontanes[97] in Italy. But howsoever it be, this matter of confederates is rather to be thought on than reckoned on, for God forbid England should be able to get reason of[98] France without a second.

'At the battles of Cressy, Poitiers, Agincourt, we were of ourselves. France has much people, and few soldiers: they have no stable bands of foot. Some good horse they have, but those are forces that are least fit for a defensive war, where the actions are in the assailant's choice. It was our discords only that lost France, and (by the power of God) it is the good peace that we now enjoy that will recover it. God has hitherto blessed my sword. I have in this time that I have reigned, weeded out my bad subjects and tried my good. My people and I know one another, which breeds confidence. And if there should be any bad blood left in the kingdom, an honourable foreign war will vent or purify it. In this great business let me have your advice and aid. If any of you were to make his son knight, you might have aid of your tenants by law. This concerns the knighthood and spurs of the kingdom, whereof I am father, and bound not only to seek to maintain it but to advance it. But for matter of treasure, let it not be taken from the poorest sort but from those to whom the benefit of the war may redound. France is no wilderness, and I that profess good husbandry hope to make the war (after the beginnings) to pay itself. Go together in God's name, and lose no time, for I have called this parliament wholly for this cause.'

Thus spoke the king. But for all this, though he showed great forwardness for a war, not only to his parliament and court but to his privy council likewise (except the two bishops[99] and a few more), yet nevertheless in his secret intentions he had no purpose to go through with any war upon France. But the truth was, that he did but traffic with that war, to make his return in money. He knew well that France was now entire and at unity with itself, and never so mighty for many years before. He saw, by the taste he had of his forces sent into Brittany, that the French knew well enough how to make war with the English, by not putting things to the hazard of a battle but wearying them by long sieges of towns and strong fortified encampings. James the Third of Scotland, his true friend and confederate, gone; and James the Fourth (that had succeeded) wholly at the devotion of France, and ill-affected towards him. As for the conjunctions of Ferdinando of Spain and Maximilian, he could make no foundation upon them. For the one had power and not will, and the other had will and not power. Besides, that Ferdinando had but newly taken breath from the war with the Moors, and merchanded at this time with France for the restoring of the counties of Roussillon and Perpignan, oppignorated to the French. Neither was he out of fear of the discontents and ill blood within the realm, which having used always to repress and appease in person, he was loath they should find him at a distance beyond sea, and engaged in war. Finding therefore the inconveniencies and difficulties in the prosecution of a war, he cast with himself how to compass two things. The one, how by the declaration and inchoation of a war to make his profit. The other, how to come off from the war with saving of his honour. For profit, it was to be made two ways: upon his subjects for the war, and upon his enemies for the peace, like a good merchant, that makes his gain both upon the commodities exported and imported back again. For the point of honour, wherein he might suffer for giving over the war, he considered well that as he could not trust upon the aids of Ferdinando and Maximilian for supports of war, so the impuissance of the one, and the double proceeding of the other, lay fair for him for occasions to accept of peace.

These things he did wisely foresee, and did as artificially conduct, whereby all things fell into his lap as he desired.

For as for the parliament, it presently took fire, being affectionate (of old) to the war of France, and desirous (afresh) to repair the dishonour they thought the King sustained by the loss of Brittany. Therefore they advised the King, with great alacrity, to undertake the war of France. And although the parliament consisted of the first and second nobility,[100] together with principal citizens and townsmen, yet worthily and justly respecting more the people (whose deputies they were) than their own private persons, and finding, by the Lord Chancellor's speech, the King's inclination that way, they consented that commissioners should go forth for the gathering and levying of a benevolence from the more able sort. This tax (called a benevolence) was devised by Edward the Fourth, for which he sustained much envy. It was abolished by Richard the Third by act of parliament, to ingratiate himself with the people, and it was now revived by the King, but with consent of parliament, for so it was not in the time of King Edward the Fourth. But ˙ this way he raised exceeding great sums. Insomuch as the city of ᴖn (in those days) contributed 9,000 pounds and better, and that chiefly levied upon the wealthier sort. There is a tradition of a dilemma that Bishop Morton (the Chancellor) used to raise up the benevolence to higher rates, and some called it his fork, and some his crotch. For he had couched an article in the instructions to the commissioners who were to levy the benevolence, that if they met with any that were sparing, they should tell them that they must needs have, because they laid up,[101] and if they were spenders, they must needs have, because it was seen in their port and manner of living; so neither kind came amiss.

This parliament was merely a parliament of war, for it was in substance but a declaration of war against France and Scotland, with some statutes conducing thereunto, as the severe punishing of mort-pays[102] and keeping back soldiers' wages in captains; the like severity for the departure of soldiers without licence; strengthening of the common law in favour of protections for those that were in the King's service; and the setting the gate open and wide, for men to sell or mortgage their lands without fines for alienation to furnish themselves with money for the war;[103] and lastly the voiding of all Scotchmen out of England.

There was also a statute for the dispersing of the standard of the exchequer[104] throughout England, thereby to size weights and measures, and two or three more of less importance.

After the parliament was broken up (which lasted not long) the King went on with his preparations for the war of France, yet neglected not in the meantime the affairs of Maximilian, for the quieting of Flanders and restoring him to his authority amongst his subjects. For at that time the Lord of Ravenstein, being not only a subject rebelled but a servant revolted (and so much the more malicious and violent), by the aid of Bruges and Ghent had taken the town and both the castles of Sluice, as we said before. And having by the commodity of the haven gotten together certain ships and barks, fell to a kind of piratical trade, robbing and spoiling and taking prisoners the ships and vessels of all nations that passed alongst that coast towards the mart of Antwerp, or into any part of Brabant, Zealand, or Friesland, being ever well victualled from Picardy, besides the commodity of victuals from Sluice and the country adjacent, and the avails of his own prizes. The French assisted him still underhand and he likewise (as all men do that have been on both sides) thought himself not safe except he depended upon a third person.

There was a small town some two miles from Bruges towards the sea, called Dam, which was a fort and approach to Bruges, and had a relation also to Sluice. This town the King of the Romans had attempted often (not for any worth of the town in itself, but because it might choke Bruges, and cut it off from the sea), and ever failed. But therewith the Duke of Saxony came down into Flanders, taking upon him the person of an umpire to compose things between Maximilian and his subjects, but being (indeed) fast and assured to Maximilian. Upon this pretext of neutrality and treaty he repaired to Bruges, desiring of the states of Bruges to enter peaceably into their town, with a retinue of some number of men of arms fit for his estate, being somewhat the more (as he said) the better to guard him in a country that was up in arms, and bearing them in hand[105] that he was to communicate with them divers matters of great importance for their good; which having obtained of them, he sent his carriages and harbingers before him to provide his lodging, so that his men of war entered the city in good array, but in peaceable manner, and he followed. They that went before enquired still for inns and lodgings as if they would have rested there all night, and so went on till they came to the gate that leads directly towards Dam, and they of Bruges only gazed upon them, and gave them passage. The captains and inhabitants of Dam also suspected no harm from any that passed through Bruges, and discovering forces afar off, supposed they had been some succours that were come from their friends, knowing some dangers towards them and so perceiving nothing but well till it was too late, suffered them to enter their town. By which kind of slight, rather than stratagem, the town of Dam was taken, and the town of Bruges shrewdly blocked up, whereby they took great discouragement.

The Duke of Saxony, having won the town of Dam, sent immediately to the King to let him know that it was Sluice chiefly and the Lord Ravenstein that kept the rebellion of Flanders in life, and that if it pleased the King to besiege it by sea, he also would besiege it by land, and so cut out the core of those wars.

The King, willing to uphold the authority of Maximilian (the better to hold France in awe), and being likewise sued unto by his merchants, for that the seas were much infested by the barks of the Lord Ravenstein, sent straightways Sir Edward Poynings, a valiant man and of good service, with twelve ships well furnished with soldiers and artillery, to clear the seas and to besiege Sluice on that part. The Englishmen did not only coop up the Lord Ravenstein, that he stirred not, and likewise held in strait siege the maritime part of the town, but also assailed one of the castles, and renewed the assault so for twenty days' space (issuing still out of their ships at the ebb), as they made great slaughter of them of the castle, who continually fought with them to repulse them, though of the English part also were slain a brother of the Earl of Oxford's, and some fifty more.

But the siege still continuing, more and more strait; and both the castles (which were the principal strength of the town) being distressed, the one by the Duke of Saxony, and the other by the English; and a bridge of boats, which the Lord Ravenstein had made between both castles, whereby succours and relief might pass from the one to the other, being on a night set on fire by the English; he despairing to hold the town, yielded (at the last) the castles to the English, and the town to the Duke of Saxony, by composition. Which done, the Duke of Saxony and Sir Edward Poynings treated with them of Bruges to submit themselves to Maximilian their lord, which after some time they did, paying (in some good part) the charge of the war, whereby the Almains and foreign succours were dismissed. The example of Bruges other of the revolted towns followed, so that Maximilian grew to be out of danger, but (as his manner was to handle matters) never out of necessity. And Edward Poynings (after he had continued at Sluice some good while, till all things were settled) returned unto the King, being then before Boulogne.

Somewhat about this time came letters from Ferdinando and Isabella, King and Queen of Spain, signifying the final conquest of Granada from the Moors; which action, in itself so worthy, King Ferdinando (whose manner was never to lose any virtue for the showing) had expressed and displayed in his letters at large, with all the particularities and religious punctos and ceremonies that were observed in the reception of that city and kingdom: showing amongst other things, that the King would not by any means in person enter the city until he had first aloof seen the cross set up upon the greater tower of Granada, whereby it became Christian ground; that likewise before he would enter he did homage to God above, pronouncing by a herald from the height of that tower that he did acknowledge to have recovered that kingdom by the help of God Almighty, and the glorious Virgin, and the virtuous Apostle St James,[106] and the holy father Innocent the Eighth, together with the aids and services of his prelates, nobles, and commons; that yet he stirred not from his camp till he had seen a little army of martyrs, to the number of 700 and more Christians (that had lived in bonds and servitude as slaves to the Moors), pass before his eyes, singing a psalm for their redemption; and that he had given tribute unto God, by alms and relief extended to them all for his admission into the city. These things were in the letters, with many more ceremonies of a kind of holy ostentation.

The King ever willing to put himself into the consort or quire of all religious actions, and naturally affecting much the King of Spain (as far as one king can affect another), partly for his virtue and partly for a counterpoise to France, upon the receipt of these letters sent all his nobles and prelates that were about the court, together with the Mayor and Aldermen of London, in great solemnity to the Church of Paul's, there to hear a declaration from the Lord Chancellor, now cardinal. When they were assembled, the Cardinal, standing upon the uppermost step or half-pace before the quire, and all the nobles, prelates, and governors of the city at the foot of the stairs, made a speech to them, letting them know that they were assembled in that consecrated place to sing unto God a new song. 'For that' (said he) 'these many years the Christians have not gained new ground or territory upon the Infidels, nor enlarged and set further the bounds of the Christian world. But this is now done by the prowess and devotion of Ferdinando and Isabella, kings of Spain, who have to their immortal honour recovered the great and rich kingdom of Granada and the populous and mighty city of the same name from the Moors, having been in possession thereof by the space of 700 years and more; for which this assembly and all Christians are to render all laud and thanks unto God, and to celebrate this noble act of the King of Spain, who in this is not only victorious but apostolical, in the gaining of new provinces to the Christian faith; and the rather for that this victory and conquest is obtained without much effusion of blood; whereby it is to be hoped that there shall be gained not only new territory, but infinite souls to the church of Christ; whom the Almighty (as it seems) would have live to be converted.' Herewithal he did relate some of the most memorable particulars of the war and victory. And after his speech ended, the whole assembly went solemnly in procession, and *Te Deum* was sung.

Immediately after the solemnity, the King kept his May Day of his palace at Sheen (now Richmond), where to warm the blood of his nobility and gallants against the war, he kept great triumphs of jousting and tourney during all that month. In which space it so fell out that Sir James Parker and Hugh Vaughan, one of the King's gentlemen ushers, having had a controversy touching certain arms that the king-at-arms had given Vaughan, were appointed to run some courses one against another, and by accident of a faulty helmet that Parker had on, he was stricken into the mouth at the first course, so that his tongue was borne unto the hinder part of his head, in such sort that he died presently upon the place, which because of controversy precedent, and the death that followed, was accounted amongst the vulgar as a combat or trial of right.

The King towards the end of this summer, having put his forces wherewith he meant to invade France in readiness (but so as they were not yet met or mustered together), sent Urswick, now made his almoner, and Sir John Risley to Maximilian, to let him know that he was in arms, ready to pass the seas into France, and did but expect to hear from him when and where he did appoint to join with him, according to his promise made unto him by Countebalt his ambassador.

The English ambassadors having repaired to Maximilian did find his power and promise at a very great distance, he being utterly unprovided of men, money, and arms for any such enterprise. For Maximilian having neither wing to fly on, for that his patrimony of Austria was not in his hands (his father being then living), and the other side his matrimonial territories of Flanders were partly in dower to his mother-in-law,[107] and partly not serviceable in respect of the late rebellions, was thereby destitute of means to enter into war. The ambassadors saw this well, but wisely thought fit to advertise the King thereof rather than to return themselves, till the King's further pleasure were known; the rather, for that Maximilian himself spoke as great as ever he did before, and entertained them with dilatory answers, so as the formal part of their ambassage might well warrant and require their further stay. The King hereupon, who doubted as much before, and saw through his business from the beginning, wrote back to the ambassadors, commending their discretion in not returning and willing them to keep the state wherein they found Maximilian as a secret, till they heard further from him, and meanwhile went on with his voyage royal for France, suppressing for a time this advertisement touching Maximilian's poverty and disability.

By this time was drawn together a great and puissant army unto the city of London, in which were Thomas Marquis Dorset, Thomas Earl of Arundel, Thomas Earl of Derby, George Earl of Shrewsbury, Edmond Earl of Suffolk, Edward Earl of Devonshire, George Earl of Kent, the Earl of Essex, Thomas Earl of Ormond with a great number of barons, knights, and principal gentlemen, and amongst them Richard Thomas, much noted for the brave troops that he brought out of Wales; the army rising in the whole to the number of five and twenty thousand foot, and sixteen hundred horse, over which the King (constant in his accustomed trust and employment) made Jasper Duke of Bedford and John Earl of Oxford generals under his own person. The ninth of September, in the eighth year of his reign, he departed from Greenwich towards the sea, all men wondering that he took that season (being so near winter) to begin the war, and some thereupon gathering it was a sign that the war would not be long. Nevertheless the King gave out the contrary, thus, that he intending not to make a summer business of it but a resolute war (without term prefixed) until he had recovered France, it skilled not much when he began it, especially having Calais at his back, where he might winter if the reason of the war so required. The sixth of October he embarked at Sandwich, and the same day took land at Calais, which was the rendezvous where all his forces were assigned to meet. But in this his journey towards the seaside, wherein for the cause that we shall now speak of he hovered so much the longer, he had received letters from the Lord Cordes (who the hotter he was against the English in time of war, had the more credit in a negotiation of peace, and besides was held a man open and of good faith), in which letters there was made an overture of peace from the French King, with such conditions as were somewhat to the King's taste; but this was carried at the first with wonderful secrecy.

The King was no sooner come to Calais but the calm winds of peace began to blow. For first the English ambassadors returned out of Flanders from Maximilian, and certified the King that he was not to hope for any aid from Maximilian, for that he was altogether unprovided. His will was good, but he lacked money. And this was made known and spread throughout the army. And although the English were therewithal nothing dismayed, and that it be the manner of soldiers upon bad news to speak the more bravely, yet nevertheless it was a kind of preparative to a peace. Instantly in the neck of this (as the King had laid it) came news that Ferdinando and Isabella, Kings of Spain, had concluded a peace with King Charles, and that Charles had restored unto them the counties of Roussillon and Perpignan, which formerly were mortgaged by John King of Aragon, Ferdinando's father, unto France, for 300,000 crowns, which debt was also upon this peace by Charles clearly released. This came also handsomely to put on the peace, both because so potent a confederate was fallen off, and because it was a fair example of the peace bought, so as the King should not be the sole merchant in this peace. Upon these airs of peace the King was content that the Bishop of Exeter and the Lord Daubeney (Governor of Calais) should give a meeting unto the Lord Cordes for the treaty of a peace; but himself nevertheless and his army, the fifteenth of October, removed from Calais, and in four days' march sat him down before Boulogne.

During this siege of Boulogne (which continued near a month) there passed no memorable action nor accident of war. Only Sir John Savage, a valiant captain, was slain, riding about the walls of the town to take a view. The town was both well fortified and well manned, yet it was distressed, and ready for an assault, which if it had been given (as was thought) would have cost much blood, but yet the town would have been carried in the end.

Meanwhile a peace was concluded by the commissioners, to continue for both the kings' lives. Where there was no article of importance, being in effect rather a bargain than a treaty. For all things remained as they were, save that there should be paid to the King

745,000 ducats in present, for his charges in that journey, and 25,000 crowns yearly, for his charges sustained in the aids of the Bretons. For which annual, though he had Maximilian bound before for those charges, yet he counted the alteration of the hand as much as the principal debt;[108] and besides it was left somewhat indefinitely when it should determine or expire, which made the English esteem it as a tribute carried under fair terms. And the truth is, it was paid both to the King and to his son Henry the Eighth longer than it could continue upon any computation of charges. There was also assigned by the French King unto all the King's principal counsellors great pensions, besides rich gifts for the present, which whether the King did permit to save his own purse from rewards, or to communicate the envy of a business that was displeasing to his people, was diversely interpreted; for certainly the King had no great fancy to own this peace, and therefore a little before it was concluded he had underhand procured some of his best captains and men of war to advise him to a peace under their hands, in an earnest manner, in the nature of a supplication.

But the truth is, this peace was welcome to both kings: to Charles, for that it assured unto him the possession of Brittany, and freed the enterprise of Naples; to Henry, for that it filled his coffers, and that he foresaw at that time a storm of inward troubles coming upon him, which presently after broke forth. But it gave no less discontent to the nobility and principal persons of the army, who had many of them sold or engaged their estates upon the hopes of the war. They stuck not to say, that the King cared not to plume his nobility and people, to feather himself. And some made themselves merry with that the King had said in parliament, that after the war was once begun, he doubted not but to make it pay itself, saying he had kept promise.

Having risen from Boulogne he went to Calais, where he stayed some time, from whence also he writ letters (which was a courtesy that he sometimes used) to the Mayor of London and the Aldermen his brethren, half bragging what great sums he had obtained for the peace, knowing well that full coffers of the King is ever good news to London, and better news it would have been, if their benevolence had been but a loan. And upon the seventeenth of September following he returned to Westminster, where he kept his Christmas.

Soon after the King's return he sent the Order of the Garter to Alphonso Duke of Calabria, eldest son to Ferdinando King of Naples. An honour sought by that prince to hold him up in the eyes of the Italians, who, expecting the arms of Charles, made great account of the amity of England for a bridle to France. It was received by Alphonso with all the ceremony and pomp that could be devised, as things use to be[109] carried that are intended for opinion. It was sent by Urswick, upon whom the King bestowed this ambassage to help him after many dry employments.

At this time the King began again to be haunted with sprites by the magic and curious arts of the Lady Margaret, who raised up the ghost of Richard Duke of York (second son to King Edward the Fourth) to walk and vex the King. This was a finer counterfeit stone than Lambert Simnel, better done, and worn upon greater hands, being graced after with the wearing of a king of France and a king of Scotland, not of a duchess of Burgundy only. And for Simnel, there was not much in him, more than that he was a handsome boy and did not shame his robes. But this youth of whom we are now to speak was such a mercurial, as the like has seldom been known, and could make his own part if any time he chanced to be out. Wherefore this being one of the strangest examples of a personation that ever was in elder or later times, it deserves to be discovered and related at the full; although the King's manner of showing things by pieces, and dark lights, has so muffled it that it has left it almost as a mystery to this day.

The Lady Margaret, whom the King's friends called Juno because she was to him as Juno was to Aeneas, stirring both heaven and hell to do him mischief, for a foundation of her particular practices against him did continually by all means possible nourish, maintain, and divulge the flying opinion that Richard Duke of York (second son to Edward the Fourth) was not murdered in the Tower (as was given out) but saved alive, for that those who were employed in that barbarous fact, having destroyed the elder brother, were stricken with remorse and compassion towards the younger, and set him privily at liberty to seek his fortune. This lure she cast abroad, thinking that this fame and belief (together with the fresh example of Lambert Simnel) would draw at one time or other some birds to strike upon it. She used likewise a further diligence, not committing all to chance, for she had some secret espials (like to the Turks' commissioners, for children of tribute[110]) to look abroad for handsome and graceful youths to make Plantagenets and dukes of York. At the last she did light on one in whom all things met as one would wish, to serve her turn for a counterfeit of Richard Duke of York.

This was Perkin Warbeck, whose adventures we shall now describe. For first, the years agreed well. Secondly, he was a youth of fine favour and shape; but more than that, he had such a crafty and bewitching fashion both to move pity and to induce belief, as was like a kind of fascination and enchantment to those that saw him or heard him. Thirdly, he had been from his childhood such a wanderer or (as the King called it) such a landloper, as it was extreme hard to hunt out his nest and parents; neither again could any man by company or conversing with him be able to say or detect well what he was, he did so flit from place to place. Lastly, there was a circumstance (which is mentioned by one that writ in the same time) that is very likely to have made somewhat to the matter, which is, that King Edward the Fourth was his godfather. Which, as it is somewhat suspicious for a wanton prince to become gossip in so mean a house, and might make a man think that he might indeed have in him some base blood of the house of York; so at the least (though that were not) it might give the occasion to the boy, in being called King Edward's godson, or perhaps in sport King Edward's son, to entertain such thoughts into his head. For tutor he had none (for ought that appears), as Lambert Simnel had, until he came unto the Lady Margaret who instructed him.

Thus therefore it came to pass. There was a townsman of Tournay that had borne office in that town, whose name was John Osbeck (a converted Jew), married to Katherine de Faro, whose business drew him to live for a time with his wife at London in King Edward the Fourth's days. During which time he had a son by her; and being known in court, the King either out of religious nobleness, because he was a convert, or upon some private acquaintance, did him the honour as to be godfather to his child, and named him Peter. But afterwards proving a dainty and effeminate youth, he was commonly called by the diminutive of his name, Peterkin or Perkin. For as for the name of Warbeck, it was given him when they did but guess at it, before examinations had been taken. But yet he had been so much talked on by that name, as it stuck by him after his true name of Osbeck was known. While he was a young child, his parents returned with him to Tournay. Then was he placed in a house of a kinsman of his, called John Stenbeck, at Antwerp, and so roamed up and down between Antwerp and Tournay and other towns of Flanders for a good time, living much in English company, and having the English tongue perfect.

In which time, being grown a comely youth, he was brought by some of the espials of the Lady Margaret into her presence, who, viewing him well, and seeing that he had a face and personage that would bear a noble fortune, and finding him otherwise of a fine spirit and winning behaviour, thought she had now found a curious piece of marble to carve out an image of a duke of York. She kept him by her a great while, but with extreme secrecy. The while she instructed him by many cabinet conferences; first, in princely behaviour and gesture, teaching him how he should keep state, and yet with a modest sense of his misfortunes. Then she informed him of all the circumstances and particulars that concerned the person of Richard Duke of York, which he was to act; describing unto him the personages, lineaments, and features of the King and Queen his pretended parents, and of his brother and sisters, and divers others that were nearest him in his childhood, together with all passages, some secret, some common, that were fit for a child's memory, until the death of King Edward. Then she added the particulars of the time from the King's death until he and his brother were committed to the Tower, as well during the time he was abroad as while he was in sanctuary. As for the times while he was in the Tower, and the manner of his brother's death and his own escape, she knew they were things that a very few could control.[111] And therefore she taught him only to tell a smooth and likely tale of those matters, warning him not to vary from it.

It was agreed likewise between them what account he should give of his peregrination abroad, intermixing many things that were true and such as they knew others could testify, for the credit of the rest, but still making them to hang together with the part he was to play. She taught him likewise how to avoid sundry captious and tempting questions, which were like to be asked of him. But in this she found him of himself so nimble and shifting as she trusted much to his own wit and readiness, and therefore laboured the less in it. Lastly, she raised his thoughts with some present rewards and further promises, setting before him chiefly the glory and fortune of a crown if things went well, and a sure refuge to her court if the worst should fall.

After such time as she thought he was perfect in his lesson she began to cast with herself from what coast this blazing star should first appear, and at what time. It must be upon the horizon of Ireland, for there had the like meteor strong influence before. The time of the apparition to be when the King should be engaged into a war with France. But well she knew that whatsoever should come from her would be held suspected. And therefore, if he should go out of Flanders immediately into Ireland, she might be thought to have some hand in it. And besides, the time was not yet ripe, for the two kings were then upon terms of peace. Therefore she led about, and to put all suspicion afar off, and loath to keep him any longer by her (for that she knew secrets are not long-lived), she sent him unknown into Portugal, with the Lady Brampton, an English lady that embarked for Portugal at that time, with some *privado* of her own to have an eye upon him, and there he was to remain and to expect her further directions. In the meantime she omitted not to prepare things for his better welcome and accepting, not only in the kingdom of Ireland, but in the court of France. He continued in Portugal about a year, and by that time the King of England called his parliament (as has been said), and had declared open war against France.

Now did the sign reign, and the constellation was come under which Perkin should appear. And therefore he was straight sent unto by the Duchess to go for Ireland, according to the first designment. In Ireland he did arrive at the town of Cork. When he was thither come his own tale was (when he made his confession afterwards) that the Irishmen finding him in some good clothes, came flocking about him, and bore him down that he was the Duke of Clarence that had been there before; and after, that he was Richard the Third's base son; and lastly, that he was Richard Duke of York, second son to Edward the Fourth. But that he for his part renounced all these things, and offered to swear upon the holy Evangelists that he was no such man, till at last they forced it upon him and bade him fear nothing, and so forth. But the truth is that immediately upon his coming into Ireland he took upon him the said person of the Duke of York, and drew unto him complices and partakers by all the means he could devise. Insomuch as he writ his letters unto the Earls of Desmond and Kildare to come in to his aid and be of his party, the originals of which letters are yet extant.

Somewhat before this time the Duchess had also gained unto her a near servant of King Henry's own, one Stephen Fryon, his secretary for the French tongue; an active man, but turbulent and discontented. This Fryon had fled over to Charles the French King, and put himself into his service at such time as he began to be in open enmity with the King. Now King Charles, when he understood of the person and attempts of Perkin, ready of himself to embrace all advantages against the King of England, instigated by Fryon, and formerly prepared by the Lady Margaret, forthwith despatched one Lucas and this Fryon in nature of ambassadors to Perkin, to advertise him of the King's good inclination to him, and that he was resolved to aid him to recover his right against King Henry, a usurper of England and an enemy of France; and wished him to come over unto him at Paris.

Perkin thought himself in heaven, now that he was invited by so great a king in so honourable a manner. And imparting unto his friends in Ireland for their encouragement how fortune called him, and what great hopes he had, sailed presently into France. When he was come to the court of France the King received him with great honour, saluted and styled him by the name of the Duke of York, lodged him and accommodated him in great state; and the better to give him the representation and the countenance of a prince, assigned him a guard for his person, whereof the Lord Congresall was captain. And the courtiers likewise (though it be ill mocking with the French[112]) applied themselves to the King's bent, seeing there was reason of state for it. At the same time there repaired unto Perkin divers Englishmen of quality: Sir George Neville, Sir John Taylor, and about one hundred more; and amongst the rest, this Stephen Fryon of whom we spoke, who followed his fortune both then and for a long time after, and was indeed his principal counsellor and instrument in proceedings.

But all this on the French King's part was but a trick, the better to bow King Henry to peace. And therefore upon the first grain of incense that was sacrificed upon the altar of peace at Boulogne, Perkin was smoked away. Yet would not the French King deliver him up to King Henry (as he was laboured to do), for his honour's sake, but warned him away and dismissed him. And Perkin on his part was as ready to be gone, doubting he might be caught up underhand. He therefore took his way into Flanders unto the Duchess of Burgundy, pretending that having been variously tossed by fortune he directed his course thither as to a safe harbour, no ways taking knowledge that he had ever been there before, but as if that had been his first address. The Duchess on the other part made it as new and strange to see him, and pretending at the first she was taught and made wise by the example of Lambert Simnel, how she did admit of any counterfeit stuff, though even in that she said she was not fully satisfied, she pretended at the first (and that was ever in the presence of others) to pose him and sift him, thereby to try whether he were indeed the very Duke of York or no. But seeming to receive full satisfaction by his answers, then she feigned herself to be transported with a kind of astonishment, mixed of joy and wonder, of his miraculous deliverance, receiving him as if he were risen from death to life, and inferring that God, who had in such wonderful manner preserved him from death, did likewise reserve him for some great and prosperous fortune. As for his dismission out of France, they interpreted it not as if he were detected or neglected for a counterfeit deceiver, but contrariwise, that it did show manifestly unto the world that he was some great matter, for that it was his abandoning that (in effect) made the peace, being no more but the sacrificing of a poor distressed prince unto the utility and ambition of two mighty monarchs.

Neither was Perkin for his part wanting to himself either in gracious and princely behaviour, or in ready and apposite answers, or in contenting and caressing those that did apply themselves unto him, or in pretty scorns or disdains to those that seemed to doubt of him; but in all things did notably acquit himself, insomuch as it was generally believed, as well amongst great persons as amongst the vulgar, that he was indeed Duke Richard. Nay himself, with long and continual counterfeiting and with often telling a lie, was turned (by habit) almost into the thing he seemed to be, and from a liar to a believer. The

Duchess therefore, as in a case out of doubt, did him all princely honour, calling him always by the name of her nephew, and giving him the delicate title of the White Rose of England, and appointed him a guard of thirty persons, halberdiers, clad in a party-coloured livery of murrey and blue, to attend his person. Her court likewise, and generally the Dutch and strangers, in their usage towards him expressed no less respect.

The news hereof came blazing and thundering over into England, that the Duke of York was sure alive. As for the name of Perkin Warbeck, it was not at that time come to light, but all the news ran upon the Duke of York, that he had been entertained in Ireland, bought and sold in France, and was now plainly avowed and in great honour in Flanders. These fames took hold of divers: in some upon discontent, in some upon ambition, in some upon levity and desire of change, and in some few upon conscience and belief, but in most upon simplicity, and in divers out of dependence upon some of the better sort who did in secret favour and nourish these bruits. And it was not long ere these rumours of novelty had begotten others of scandal and murmur against the King and his government, taxing him for a great taxer of his people and discountenancer of his nobility. The loss of Brittany and the peace with France were not forgotten, but chiefly they fell upon the wrong that he did his Queen, and that he did not reign in her right, wherefore they said that God had now brought to light a masculine branch of the house of York that would not be at his courtesy, howsoever he did depress his poor lady. And yet (as it fares in things that are current with the multitude, and which they affect) these fames grew so general as the authors were lost in the generality of speakers, they being like running weeds that have no certain root, or like footings up and down[113] impossible to be traced.

But after a while these ill humours drew to a head, and settled secretly in some eminent persons, which were Sir William Stanley, Lord Chamberlain of the King's household, the Lord Fitzwater, Sir Symon Mountfort, Sir Thomas Thwaites. These entered into a secret conspiracy to favour Duke Richard's title; nevertheless none engaged their fortunes in this business openly but two, Sir Robert Clifford and master William Barley, who sailed over into Flanders, sent indeed from the party of the conspirators here to understand the truth of those things that passed there, and not without some help of moneys from hence, provisionally to be delivered – if they found and were satisfied that there was truth in these pretences. The person of Sir Robert Clifford (being a gentleman of fame and family) was extremely welcome to the Lady Margaret, who after she had conference with him brought him to the sight of Perkin, with whom he had often speech and discourse. So that in the end, won either by the Duchess to affect or by Perkin to believe, he wrote back into England that he knew the person of Richard Duke of York as well as he knew his own, and that this young man was undoubtedly he. By this means all things grew prepared to revolt and sedition here, and the conspiracy came to have a correspondence between Flanders and England.

The King on his part was not asleep. But to arm or levy forces yet, he thought he would but show fear, and do this idol too much worship. Nevertheless the ports he did shut up, or at least kept a watch on them, that none should pass to or fro that was suspected. But for the rest he chose to work by countermine. His purposes were two: the one to lay open the abuse, the other to break the knot of the conspirators. To detect the abuse, there were but two ways: the first to make it manifest to the world that the Duke of York was indeed murdered; the other to prove that, were he dead or alive, yet Perkin was a counterfeit. For the first, thus it stood. There were but four persons that could speak upon knowledge to the murder of the Duke of York: Sir James Tyrell (the employed man from King Richard), John Dighton and Myles Forrest his servants (the two butchers or tormentors), and the priest of the Tower that buried them. Of which four, Myles Forrest and the priest were dead, and there remained alive only Sir James Tyrell and John Dighton. These two the King caused to be committed to the Tower and examined touching the manner of the death of the two innocent princes.

They agreed both in a tale (as the King gave out) to this effect: that King Richard having directed his warrant for the putting of them to death to Brackenbury, the Lieutenant of the Tower, was by him refused. Whereupon the King directed his warrant to Sir James Tyrell to receive the keys of the Tower from the lieutenant (for the space of a night) for the King's especial service. That Sir James Tyrell accordingly repaired to the Tower by night, attended by his two servants afore-named, whom he had chosen for the purpose. That himself stood at the stair foot and sent these two villains to execute the murder. That they smothered them in their bed, and, that done, called up their master to see the naked bodies dead, which they had laid forth. That they were buried under the stairs, and some stones cast upon them. That when the report was made to King Richard that his will was done, he gave Sir James Tyrell great thanks, but took exception to the place of their burial, being too base for them that were king's children. Whereupon another night, by the King's warrant renewed, their bodies were removed by the priest of the Tower, and buried by him in some place which, by means of the priest's death soon after, could not be known. Thus much was then delivered abroad, to be the effect of those examinations, but the King nevertheless made no use of them in any of his declarations. Whereby, as it seems, those examinations left the business somewhat perplexed. And as for Sir James Tyrell, he was long after beheaded in the Tower yard for other matters of treason. But John Dighton, who it seems spoke best for the King, was forthwith set at liberty, and was the principal means of divulging this tradition.

Therefore this kind of proof being left so naked, the King used the more diligence in the latter for the tracing of Perkin. To this purpose he sent abroad into several parts, and especially into Flanders, divers secret and nimble scouts and spies, some feigning themselves to fly over unto Perkin and to adhere unto him, and some under other pretences to learn, search, and discover all the circumstances and particulars of Perkin's parents, birth, person, travels up and down, and in brief, to have a journal (as it were) of his life and doings; and furnished these his employed men liberally with money to draw on and reward intelligences, giving them also in charge to advertise continually what they found, and nevertheless still to go on. And ever as one advertisement and discovery called up another, he employed other new men where the business did require it.

Others he employed in a more special nature and trust, to be his pioners[114] in the main countermine. These were directed to insinuate themselves into the familiarity and confidence of the principal persons of the party in Flanders, and so to learn what associates they had and correspondents, either here in England or abroad, and how far everyone was engaged, and what new ones they meant afterwards to try or board; and as this for the persons, so for the actions themselves, to discover to the bottom (as they could) the utmost of Perkin and the conspirators their intentions, hopes, and practices. These latter best betrust spies had some of them further instructions, to practise and draw off the best friends and servants of Perkin by making remonstrance to them how weakly his enterprise and hopes were built, and with how prudent and potent a king they had to deal, and to reconcile them to the King with promise of pardon and good conditions of reward. And above the rest to assail, sap, and work into the constancy of Sir Robert Clifford, and to win him (if they could), being the man that knew most of their secrets, and who being won away would most appal and discourage the rest, and in a manner break the knot.

There is a strange tradition that the King, lost in a wood of suspicions, and not knowing whom to trust, had both intelligence with the confessors and chaplains of divers great men; and for the better credit of his espials abroad with the contrary side, did use to have them cursed at Paul's (by name) amongst the bead-roll of the King's enemies, according to the custom of those times. These spials plied their charge so roundly, as the King had an anatomy of Perkin alive, and was likewise well informed of the particular correspondent conspirators in England, and many other mysteries were revealed; and Sir Robert Clifford in especial won to be assured to the King, and industrious and officious for his service. The King therefore, receiving a rich return of his diligence, and great satisfaction touching a number of particulars, first divulged and spread abroad the imposture and juggling of Perkin's person and travels, with the circumstances thereof, throughout the realm; not by proclamation (because things were yet in examination, and so might receive the more or the less), but by court-fames, which commonly print better than printed proclamations. Then thought he it also time to send an ambassage unto Archduke Philip[115] into Flanders for the abandoning and dismissing of Perkin. Herein he employed Sir Edward Poynings and Sir William Warham,[116] doctor of the canon law. The Archduke was then young and governed by his council, before whom the ambassadors had audience. And Dr Warham spoke in this manner:

'My lords, the King our master is very sorry that England and your country here of Flanders, having been counted as man and wife for so long time, now this country of all others should be the stage where a base counterfeit should play the part of a king of England, not only to his grace's disquiet and dishonour but to the scorn and reproach of all sovereign princes. To counterfeit the dead image of a king in his coin is a high offence by all laws. But to counterfeit the living image of a king in his person exceeds all falsifications, except it should be that of a Mahomet or an Antichrist, that counterfeit divine honour. The King has too great an opinion of this sage council to think that any of you is caught with this fable (though way may be given by you[117] to the passion of some), the thing in itself is so improbable. To set testimonies aside of the death of Duke Richard, which the King has upon record plain and infallible, because they may be thought to be in the King's own power,[118] let the thing testify for itself. Sense and reason no power can command. Is it possible (trow you) that King Richard should damn his soul and foul his name with so abominable a murder, and yet not mend his case? Or do you think that men of blood (that were his instruments) did turn to pity in the midst of their execution? whereas in cruel and savage beasts, and men also, the first draught of blood does yet make them more fierce and enraged. Do you not know that the bloody executioners of tyrants do go to such errands with a halter about their neck, so that if they perform not they are sure to die for it? And do you think that these men would hazard their own lives for sparing another's? Admit they should have saved him, what should they have done with him? Turn him into London streets? that the watchmen, or any passenger that should light upon him, might carry him before justice, and so all come to light? Or should they have kept him by them secretly? That surely would have required a great deal of care, charge, and continual fears.

'But, my lords, I labour too much in a clear business. The King is so wise, and has so good friends abroad, as now he knows Duke Perkin from his cradle. And because he is a great prince, if you have any good poet here, he can help him with notes to write his life, and to parallel him with Lambert Simnel, now the King's falconer. And therefore, to speak plainly to your lordships, it is the strangest thing in the world that the Lady Margaret (excuse us if we name her, whose malice to the King is both causeless and endless), should now when she is old, at the time when other women give over childbearing, bring forth two such monsters being not the births of nine or ten months but of many years. And whereas other natural mothers bring forth children weak, and not able to help themselves, she brings forth tall striplings, able soon after their coming into the world to bid battle to mighty kings. My lords, we stay unwillingly upon this part: we would to God that lady would once taste the joys that God Almighty does serve up unto her, in beholding her niece to reign in such honour and with so much royal issue, which she might be pleased to account as her own. The King's request unto the Archduke and your lordships might be, that according to the example of King Charles, who has already discarded him, you would banish this unworthy fellow out of your dominions. But because the King may justly expect more from an ancient confederate than from a new reconciled enemy, he makes it his request unto you to deliver him up into his hands, pirates and impostors of this sort being fit to be accounted the common enemies of mankind, and no ways to be protected by the law of nations.'

After some time of deliberation, the ambassadors received this short answer: 'That the Archduke, for the love of King Henry, would in no sort aid or assist the pretended Duke, but in all things conserve the amity he had with the King. But for the Duchess Dowager, she was absolute in the lands of her dowry, and that he could not let[119] her to dispose of her own.'

The King, upon the return of the ambassadors, was nothing satisfied with this answer, for well he knew that a patrimonial dowry[120] carried no part of sovereignty or command of forces. Besides, the ambassadors told him plainly that they saw the Duchess had a great party in the Archduke's counsel, and that howsoever it was carried in a course of connivance, yet the Archduke underhand gave aid and furtherance to Perkin. Wherefore (partly out of courage and partly out of policy) the King forthwith banished all Flemings, as well their persons as their wares, out of his kingdom; commanding his subjects likewise, and by name his Merchant Adventurers, which had a resiance in Antwerp to return, translating the mart (which commonly followed the English cloth) unto Calais, and embarred also all further trade for the future. This the King did, being sensible in point of honour not to suffer a pretender to the crown of England to affront him so near at hand, and he[121] to keep terms of friendship with the country where he[122] did set up. But he had also a further reach, for that he knew well that the subjects of Flanders drew so great commodity from the trade of England as by this embargo they would soon wax weary of Perkin, and that the tumults of Flanders had been so late and fresh as it was no time for the Prince to displease the people. Nevertheless for form's sake, by way of requital, the Archduke did likewise banish the English out of Flanders, which in effect was done to his hand.

The King, being well advertised that Perkin did more trust upon friends and partakers within the realm than upon foreign arms, thought it behoved him to apply the remedy where the disease lay, and to proceed with severity against some of the principal conspirators here within the realm, thereby to purge the ill humours in England and to cool the hopes in Flanders. Wherefore he caused to be apprehended, almost at an instant, John Ratcliffe Lord Fitzwater, Sir Symon Mountfort, Sir Thomas Thwaites, William Daubeney, Robert Ratcliffe, Thomas Chressenor, and Thomas Astwood. All these were arraigned, convicted, and condemned for high treason, in adhering and promising aid to Perkin. Of these the Lord Fitzwater was conveyed to Calais, and there kept in hold and in hope of life, until soon after (either impatient or betrayed) he dealt with his keeper to have escaped, and thereupon was beheaded. But Sir Symon Mountfort, Robert Ratcliffe, and William Daubeney were beheaded immediately after their condemnation. The rest were pardoned, together with many others, clerks and laics, amongst which were two Dominican friars, and William Worseley Dean of Paul's, which latter sort passed examination, but came not to public trial.

The Lord Chamberlain[123] at that time was not touched; whether it were that the King would not stir too many humours at once, but, after the manner of good physicians, purge the head last, or that Clifford (from whom most of these discoveries came) reserved that piece for his own coming over, signifying only to the King in the meantime that he doubted there were some greater ones in the business, whereof he would give the King further account when he came to his presence.

Upon Allhallows-day even, being now the tenth year of the King's reign, the King's second son Henry[124] was created Duke of York, and as well the Duke as divers others, noblemen, knights-bachelors, and gentlemen of quality, were made Knights of the Bath according to the ceremony. Upon the morrow after Twelfth-day, the King removed from Westminster (where he had kept his Christmas) to the Tower of London. This he did as soon as he had advertisement that Sir Robert Clifford (in whose bosom or budget most of Perkin's secrets were laid up) was come into England. And the place of the Tower was chosen to that end, that if Clifford should accuse any of the great ones, they might without suspicion or noise or sending abroad of warrants be presently attached,[125] the court and prison being within the cincture of one wall. After a day or two the King drew unto him a selected council, and admitted Clifford to his presence, who first fell down at his feet, and in all humble manner craved the King's pardon, which the King then granted, though he were indeed secretly assured of his life before. Then, commanded to tell his knowledge, he did amongst many others (of himself not interrogated) impeach Sir William Stanley, the Lord Chamberlain of the King's household.

The King seemed to be much amazed at the naming of this lord, as if he had heard the news of some strange and fearful prodigy. To hear a man that had done him service of so high a nature as to save his life and set the crown upon his head; a man that enjoyed by his favour and advancement so great a fortune both in honour and riches; a man that was tied unto him in so near a band of alliance, his brother having married the King's mother; and lastly a man to whom he had committed the trust of his person, in making him his chamberlain: that this man, no ways disgraced, no ways discontent, no ways put in fear, should be false unto him. Clifford was required to say over again and again the particulars of his accusation, being warned that in a matter so unlikely, and that concerned so great a servant of the King's, he should not in any wise go too far. But the King finding that he did sadly and constantly, without hesitation or varying, and with those civil protestations that were fit, stand to that that he had said, offering to justify it upon his soul and life, he caused him to be removed. And after he had not a little bemoaned himself unto his council there present, gave order that Sir William Stanley should be restrained in his own chamber, where he lay before, in the square tower. And the next day he was examined by the lords.

Upon his examination he denied little of that wherewith he was charged, nor endeavoured much to excuse or extenuate his fault. So that (not very wisely), thinking to make his offence less by confession he made it enough for condemnation. It was conceived that he trusted much to his former merits and the interest that his brother had in the King. But those helps were over-weighed by divers things that made against him, and were predominant in the King's nature and mind. First, an over-merit; for convenient merit, unto which reward may easily reach, does best with kings. Next, the sense of his power; for the King thought that he that could set him up was the more dangerous to pull him down. Thirdly, the glimmering of a confiscation; for he was the richest subject for value in the kingdom, there being found in his castle of Holte 40,000 marks in ready money and plate, besides jewels, household stuff, stocks upon his grounds, and other personal estate exceeding great, and for his revenue in land and fee it was 3,000 pounds a year of old rent, a great matter in those times. Lastly, the nature of the time; for if the King had been out of fear of his own estate it was not unlike he would have spared his life, but the cloud of so great a rebellion hanging over his head made him work sure. Wherefore after some six weeks' distance of time, which the King did honourably interpose, both to give space to his brother's intercession, and to show to the world that he had a conflict with himself what he should do, he was arraigned of high treason and condemned, and presently after beheaded.

It is yet to this day left but in dark memory both what the case of this noble person was, for which he suffered, and what likewise was the ground and cause of his defection and alienation of his heart from the King. His case was said to be this, that in discourse between Sir Robert Clifford and him he had said that if he were sure that that young man were King Edward's son, he would never bear arms against him. This case seems somewhat a hard case, both in respect of the conditional, and in respect of the other words. But for the conditional, it seems the judges of that time (who were learned men, and the three chief of them of the privy council) thought it was a dangerous thing to admit Ifs and Ands to qualify words of treason, whereby every man might express his malice, and blanch his danger. And it was like to the case (in the following times) of Elizabeth Barton, the holy maid of Kent, who had said that if King Henry the Eighth did not take Catherine his wife again, he should be deprived of his crown, and die the death of a dog. And infinite cases may be put of like nature, which it seems the grave judges taking into consideration, would not admit of treasons upon condition. And as for the positive words, that he would not bear arms against King Edward's son; though the words seem calm, yet it was a plain and direct overruling of the King's title, either by the line of Lancaster or by act of parliament, which no doubt pierced the King more than if Stanley had charged his lance upon him in the field. For if Stanley would hold that opinion, that a son of King Edward had still the better right, he being so principal a person of authority and favour about the King, it was to teach all England to say as much. And therefore, as those times were, that speech touched the quick. But some writers do put this out of doubt, for they say that Stanley did expressly promise to aid Perkin, and sent him some help of treasure.

Now for the motive of his falling off from the King. It is true that at Bosworth field the King was beset, and in a manner enclosed round about by the troops of King Richard, and in manifest danger of his life when this Stanley was sent by his brother with 3,000 men to his rescue, which he performed so that King Richard was slain upon the place. So as the condition of mortal men is not capable of a greater benefit than the King received by the hands of Stanley, being like the benefit of Christ, at once to save and crown. For which service the King gave him great gifts, made him his counsellor and chamberlain, and (somewhat contrary to his nature) had winked at the great spoils of Bosworth field, which came almost wholly to this man's hands, to his infinite enriching. Yet nevertheless, blown up with the conceit of his merit, he did not think he had received good measure from the King, at least not pressing down and running over,[126] as he expected. And his ambition was so exorbitant and unbounded as he became suitor to the King for the earldom of Chester, which ever being a kind of appanage to the principality of Wales, and using to go to the king's son, his suit did not only end in a denial but in a distaste, the King perceiving thereby that his desires were intemperate and his cogitations vast and irregular, and that his former benefits were but cheap and lightly regarded by him. Wherefore the King began not to brook him well, and as a little leaven of new distaste does commonly sour the whole lump of former merits, the King's wit began now to suggest unto his passion that Stanley at Bosworth field, though he came time enough to save his life, yet he stayed long enough to endanger it. But yet having no matter against him, he continued him in his places until this his fall.

After him was made Lord Chamberlain Giles Lord Daubeney, a man of great sufficiency and valour, the more because he was gentle and moderate.

There was a common opinion that Sir Robert Clifford (who now was become the state informer) was from the beginning an emissary and spy of the King's, and that he fled over into Flanders with his consent and privity. But this is not probable, both because he never recovered that degree of grace that he had with the King before his going over, and chiefly for that the discovery that he had made touching the Lord Chamberlain (which was his great service) grew not from anything he learned abroad, for that he knew it well before he went. These executions, and specially that of the Lord Chamberlain, which was the chief strength of the party and by means of Sir Robert Clifford who was the most inward man of trust amongst them, did extremely quail the design of Perkin and his complices, as well through discouragement as distrust. So that they were now like sand without lime, ill bound together; especially as many as were English, who were at a gaze, looking strange one upon another, not knowing who was faithful to their side but thinking that the King (what with his baits and what with his nets) would draw them all unto him that were any thing worth. And indeed it came to pass that divers came away by the thread, sometimes one and sometimes another. Barley, that was joint commissioner with Clifford, did hold out one of the longest, till Perkin was far worn, yet made his peace at length. But the fall of this great man,[127] being in so high authority and favour (as was thought) with the King, and the manner of carriage of the business, as if there had been secret inquisition upon him for a great time before, and the cause for which he suffered, which was little more than for saying in effect that the title of York was better than the title of Lancaster, which was the case almost of every man (at the least in opinion), was matter of great terror amongst all the King's servants and subjects, insomuch as no man almost thought himself secure, and men dared scarce commune or talk one with another, but there was a general diffidence everywhere, which nevertheless made the King rather absolute than more safe. For bleeding inwards and shut vapours strangle soonest and oppress most.

Hereupon presently came forth swarms and vollies of libels (which are the gusts of liberty of speech restrained, and the females of sedition), containing bitter invectives and slanders against the King and some of the council, for the contriving and dispersing whereof (after great diligence of enquiry) five mean persons were caught up and executed.

Meanwhile the King did not neglect Ireland, being the soil where these mushrooms and upstart weeds that spring up in a night did chiefly prosper. He sent therefore from hence (for the better settling of his affairs there) commissioners of both robes,[128] the Prior of Llanthony to be his Chancellor in that kingdom, and Sir Edward Poynings with a power of men and a marshal commission, together with a civil power of his Lieutenant, with a clause that the Earl of Kildare, then Deputy, should obey him. But the wild Irish, who were the principal offenders, fled into the woods and bogs, after their manner, and those that knew themselves guilty in the pale[129] fled to them. So that Sir Edward Poynings was enforced to make a wild chase upon the wild Irish, where, in respect of the mountains and fastnesses, he did little good, which (either out of a suspicious melancholy upon his bad success, or the better to save his service from disgrace), he would needs impute unto the comfort that the rebels should receive underhand from the Earl of Kildare, every light suspicion growing upon the Earl, in respect of the Kildare that was in the action of Lambert Simnel, and slain at Stokefield. Wherefore he caused the Earl to be apprehended, and sent into England, where upon examination he cleared himself so well as he was replaced in his government. But Poynings, the better to make compensation of the meagreness of his service in the wars by acts of peace, called a parliament, where was made that memorable act that at this day is called Poynings' Law, whereby all the statutes of England were made to be of force in Ireland. For before they were not; neither are any now in force in Ireland, which were made in England since that time, which was the tenth year of the King.

About this time began to be discovered in the King that disposition that afterwards, nourished and whet on by bad counsellors and ministers, proved the blot of his times, which was the course he took to crush treasure out of his subjects' purses by forfeitures upon penal laws. At this men did startle the more at this time, because it appeared plainly to be in the King's nature, and not out of his necessity, he being now in float for treasure; for that he had newly received the peace money from France, the benevolence money from his subjects, and great casualties upon the confiscations of the Lord Chamberlain and divers others. The first noted case of this kind was that of Sir William Capel, Alderman of London, who upon sundry penal laws was condemned in the sum of 720 pounds, and compounded with the King for 1,600; and yet after, Empson[130] would have cut another chop out of him if the King had not died in the instant.

The summer following, the King, to comfort his mother, whom he did always tenderly love and revere, and to make open demonstration to the world that the proceeding against Sir William Stanley (which was imposed upon him by necessity of state) had not in any degree diminished the affection he bore to Thomas his brother, went in progress to Latham, to make merry with his mother and the Earl, and lay there divers days.

During this progress Perkin Warbeck, finding that time and temporising, which while his practices were covert and wrought well in England made for him,[131] did now when they were discovered and defeated rather make against him (for that when matters once go down the hill they stay not without a new force), resolved to try his adventure in some exploit upon England, hoping still upon the affections of the common people towards the house of York. Which body of common people he thought was not to be practised upon as persons of quality are, but that the only practice upon their affections was to set up a standard in the field. The place where he should make his attempt he chose to be the coast of Kent.

The King by this time was grown to such a height of reputation for cunning and policy that every accident and event that went well was laid and imputed to his foresight, as if he had set it before. As in this particular of Perkin's design upon Kent. For the world would not believe afterwards but the King, having secret intelligence of Perkin's intention for Kent, the better to draw it on, went of purpose into the north afar off, laying an open side unto Perkin to make him come to the close, and so to trip up his heels, having made sure in Kent beforehand.

But so it was that Perkin had gathered together a power of all nations, neither in number nor in the hardiness and courage of the persons contemptible, but in their nature and fortunes to be feared well of friends as enemies, being bankrupts, and many of them felons, and such as lived by rapine. These he put to sea, and arrived upon the coast of Sandwich and Deal in Kent about July.

There he cast anchor, and to prove the affections of the people sent some of his men to land, making great boasts of the power that was to follow. The Kentish men, perceiving that Perkin was not followed by any English of name or account, and that his forces consisted but of strangers born, and most of them base people and freebooters, fitter to spoil a coast than to recover a kingdom, resorting unto the principal gentlemen of the country, professed their loyalty to the King and desired to be directed and commanded for the best of the King's service. The gentlemen, entering into consultation, directed some forces in good number to show themselves upon the coast, and some of them to make signs to entice Perkin's soldiers to land, as if they would join with them, and some others to appear from some other places, and to make semblance as if they fled from them, the better to encourage them to land. But Perkin, who by playing the Prince, or else taught by secretary Fryon, had learned thus much, that people under command do use to consult and after to march on in order, and rebels contrariwise run upon a head together in confusion, considering the delay of time, and observing their orderly and not tumultuary arming, doubted the worst. And therefore the wily youth would not set one foot out of his ship till he might see things were sure.

Wherefore the King's forces, perceiving that they could draw on no more than those that were formerly landed, set upon them and cut them in pieces ere they could fly back to their ships. In which skirmish (besides those that fled and were slain) there were taken about 150 persons, which, for that the King thought that to punish a few for example was gentleman's pay, but for rascal people they were to be cut off every man, especially in the beginning of an enterprise; and likewise for that he saw that Perkin's forces would now consist chiefly of such rabble and scum of desperate people, he therefore hanged them all for the greater terror. They were brought to London all railed in ropes, like a team of horses in a cart, and were executed some of them at London and Wapping, and the rest at divers places upon the sea coast of Kent, Sussex, and Norfolk, for sea marks or lighthouses to teach Perkin's people to avoid the coast. The King being advertised of landing of the rebels, thought to leave his progress. But being certified the next day that they were partly defeated and partly fled, continued his progress, and sent Sir Richard Guildford into Kent in message, who calling the country together, did much commend (from the King) their fidelity, manhood, and well handling of that service, and gave them all thanks, and in private promised reward to some particulars.

Upon the sixteenth of November (this being the eleventh year of the King) was held the Serjeants' feast at Ely Place, there being nine serjeants of that call.[132] The King, to honour the feast, was present with his queen at the dinner, being a prince that was ever ready to grace and countenance the professors of the law; having a little of that, that as he governed his subjects by his laws, so he governed his laws by his lawyers.

This year also the King entered into league with the Italian potentates for the defence of Italy against France. For King Charles had conquered the realm of Naples, and lost it again, in a kind of felicity of a dream. He passed the whole length of Italy without resistance, so that it was true which Pope Alexander was wont to say, that the Frenchmen came into Italy with chalk in their hands to mark up their lodgings rather than with swords to fight. He likewise entered and won in effect the whole kingdom of Naples itself without striking stroke. But presently thereupon he did commit and multiply so many errors as was too great a task for the best fortune to overcome. He gave no contentment to the barons of Naples, of the faction of the Angevins, but scattered his rewards according to the mercenary appetites of some about him. He put all Italy upon their guard, by the seizing and holding of Ostia, and the protecting of the liberty of Pisa, which made all men suspect that his purposes looked further than his title of Naples. He fell too soon at difference with Ludovico Sforza, who was the man that carried the keys that brought him in and shut him out. He neglected to extinguish some relics of the war. And lastly, in regard of his easy passage through Italy without resistance, he entered into an overmuch despising of the arms of the Italians, whereby he left the realm of Naples at his departure so much the less provided. So that not long after his return the whole kingdom revolted to Ferdinando the younger, and the French were quite driven out. Nevertheless Charles did make both great threats and great preparations to re-enter Italy once again, wherefore at the instance of divers of the states of Italy (and especially of Pope Alexander) there was a league concluded between the said Pope, Maximilian King of the Romans, Henry King of England, Ferdinando and Isabella King and Queen of Spain (for so they are constantly placed in the original treaty throughout), Augustino Barbadico Duke of Venice, and Ludovico Sforza Duke of Milan, for the common defence of their estates: wherein though Ferdinando of Naples was not named as principal, yet no doubt the kingdom of Naples was tacitly included as a fee of the church.[133]

There died also this year Cecile Duchess of York, mother to King Edward the Fourth, at her castle of Barkhamsted, being of extreme years, and who had lived to see three princes of her body crowned, and four murdered.[134] She was buried at Fotheringham, by her husband.

This year also the King called his parliament, where many laws were made of a more private and vulgar nature than ought to detain the reader of a history. And it may be justly suspected by the proceedings following, that as the King did excel in good commonwealth laws, so nevertheless he had in secret a design to make use of them as well for collecting of treasure as for correcting of manners, and so meaning thereby to harrow his people did accumulate them the rather.

The principal law that was made this parliament was a law of a strange nature, rather just than legal, and more magnanimous than provident. This law did ordain that no person that did assist (in arms or otherwise) the King for the time being, should after be impeached therefore, or attainted either by the course of law or by act of parliament, but if any such act of attainder did happen to be made, it should be void and of none effect, for that it was agreeable reason of estate that the subject should not enquire of the justness of the King's title or quarrel, and it was agreeable to good conscience that (whatsoever the fortune of the war were) the subject should not suffer for his obedience. The spirit of this law was wonderful pious and noble, being like, in matter of war, unto the spirit of David in matter of plague, who said, 'If I have sinned strike me, but what have these sheep done?'[135] Neither wanted this law parts of prudent and deep foresight. For it did the better take away occasion for the people to busy themselves to pry into the King's title, for at (howsoever it fell) their safety was already provided for. Besides, it could not but greatly draw unto him the love and hearts of the people, because he seemed more careful for them than for himself. But yet nevertheless it did take off from his party that great tie and spur of necessity to fight and go victors out of the field, considering their lives and fortunes were put in safety and protected, whether they stood to it or ran away.

But the force and obligation of this law was in itself illusory, as the latter part of it, by a precedent act of parliament to bind or frustrate a future. For a supreme and absolute power cannot conclude itself,[136] neither can that which is in nature revocable be made fixed, no more than if a man should appoint or declare by his will that if he made any later will it should be void. And for the case of the act of parliament, there is a notable precedent of it in King Henry the Eighth's time, who doubting he might die in the minority of his son, procured an act to pass that no statute made during the minority of a king should bind him or his successors, except it were confirmed by the King under his great seal at his full age. But the first act that passed in King Edward the Sixth's time was an act of repeal of that former act, at which time nevertheless the King was minor. But things that do not bind may satisfy for time.

There was also made a shoring or underpropping act for the benevolence: to make the sums that any person had agreed to pay, and nevertheless were not brought in, to be leviable by course of law. Which act did not only bring in the arrears, but did indeed countenance the whole business, and was pretended to be made at the desire of those that had been forward to pay.

This parliament also was made that good law that gave the attaint upon a false verdict between party and party, which before was a kind of evangile, irremediable.[137] It extends not to causes capital, as well because they are for the most part at the King's suit, as because in them, if they be followed in course of indictment, there passes a double jury, the indictors and the triers, and so not twelve men but four and twenty. But it seems that was not the only reason, for this reason holds not in the appeal. But the great reason was, lest it should tend to the discouragement of jurors in cases of life and death if they should be subject to suit and penalty, where the favour of life makes against them. It extended not also to any suit where the demand is under the value of forty pounds, for that in such cases of petty value it would not quit the charge to go about again.[138]

There was another law made against a branch of ingratitude in women, who having been advanced by their husbands or their husbands' ancestors, should alien and thereby seek to defeat the heirs or those in remainder of the lands whereunto they had been so advanced. The remedy was by giving power to the next[139] to enter for a forfeiture.

There was also enacted that charitable law for the admission of poor suitors *in forma pauperis*,[140] without fee to counsellor, attorney, or clerk, whereby poor men became rather able to vex than unable to sue. There were divers other good laws made that parliament, as we said before, but we still observe our manner in selecting out those that are not of a vulgar nature.

The King this while, though he sat in parliament as in full peace, and seemed to account of the designs of Perkin (who was now returned into Flanders) but as of a may-game, yet having the composition of a wise king, stout without and apprehensive within, had given order for the watching of beacons upon the coast, and erecting more where they stood too thin, and had a careful eye where this wandering cloud would break. But Perkin, advised to keep his fire (which hitherto burned as it were upon green wood) alive with continual blowing, sailed again into

Ireland, whence he had formerly departed, rather upon the hopes of France than upon any unreadiness or discouragement he found in that people. But in the space of time between, the King's diligence and Poynings' commission had so settled things there as there was nothing left for Perkin but the blustering affection of the wild and naked people. Wherefore he was advised by his council to seek aid of the King of Scotland,[141] a prince young and valorous, and in good terms with his nobles and people, and ill-affected to King Henry. At this time also both Maximilian and Charles of France began to bear no good will to the King: the one being displeased with the King's prohibition of commerce with Flanders, the other holding the King for suspect in regard of his late entry into league with the Italians. Wherefore besides the open aids of the Duchess of Burgundy, which did with sails and oars put on and advance Perkin's designs, there wanted not some secret tides from Maximilian and Charles that did further his fortunes, insomuch as they both by their secret letters and messages recommended him to the King of Scotland.

Perkin therefore coming into Scotland upon those hopes with a well-appointed company, was by the King of Scots (being formerly well prepared) honourably welcomed, and soon after his arrival admitted to his presence in a solemn manner. For the King received him in state in his chamber of presence, accompanied with divers of his nobles. And Perkin, well attended as well with those that the King had sent before him as with his own train, entered the room where the King was, and coming near to the King, and bowing a little to embrace him, he retired some paces back, and with a loud voice, that all that were present might hear him, made his declarations in this manner:

'High and mighty King; your grace and these your nobles here present may be pleased benignly to bow your ears to hear the tragedy of a young man that by right ought to hold in his hand the ball of a kingdom, but by fortune is made himself a ball, tossed from misery to misery and from place to place. You see here before you the spectacle of a Plantagenet, who has been carried from the nursery to the sanctuary, from the sanctuary to the direful prison, from the prison to the hand of the cruel tormentor, and from that hand to the wide wilderness (as I may truly call it), for so the world has been to me. So that he that is born to a great kingdom has not ground to set his foot upon, more than this where he now stands by your princely favour.

'Edward the Fourth, late King of England (as your grace cannot but have heard), left two sons, Edward and Richard Duke of York, both very young. Edward the eldest succeeded their father in the crown, by the name of King Edward the Fifth. But Richard Duke of Gloucester, their unnatural uncle, first thirsting after the kingdom through ambition, and afterwards thirsting for their blood out of desire to secure himself, employed an instrument of his (confident to him as he thought) to murder them both. But this man that was employed to execute that execrable tragedy, having cruelly slain King Edward, the eldest of the two, was moved partly by remorse and partly by some other mean to save Richard his brother, making a report nevertheless to the tyrant that he had performed his commandment for both brethren.

'This report was accordingly believed, and published generally. So that the world has been possessed of an opinion that they both were barbarously made away, though ever truth has some sparks that fly abroad until it appear in due time, as this has had. But Almighty God, that stopped the mouth of the lions, and saved little Joas from the tyranny of Athaliah when she massacred the King's children, and did save Isaac when the hand was stretched forth to sacrifice him,[142] preserved the second brother. For I myself that stand here in your presence am that very Richard Duke of York, brother of that unfortunate prince King Edward the Fifth, now the most rightful surviving heir-male to that victorious and most noble Edward, of that name the Fourth, late King of England.

'For the manner of my escape, it is fit it should pass in silence, or at least in a more secret relation, for that it may concern some alive, and the memory of some that are dead. Let it suffice to think that I had then a mother living, a queen, and one that expected daily such a commandment from the tyrant for the murdering of her children. Thus in my tender age escaping by God's mercy out of London, I was secretly conveyed over sea, where after a time the party that had me in charge (upon what new fears, change of mind, or practice, God knows) suddenly forsook me, whereby I was forced to wander abroad, and to seek mean conditions for the sustaining of my life. Wherefore distracted between several passions, the one of fear to be known, lest the tyrant should have a new attempt upon me, the other of grief and disdain to be unknown and to live in that base and servile manner that I did, I resolved with myself to expect the tyrant's death, and then to put myself into my sister's hands, who was next heir to the crown. But in this season it happened one Henry Tudor, son to Edmund Tudor Earl of Richmond, to come from France and enter into the realm, and by subtile and foul means to obtain the crown of the same, which to me rightfully appertained, so that it was but a change from tyrant to tyrant.

'This Henry, my extreme and mortal enemy, so soon as he had knowledge of my being alive, imagined and wrought all the subtile ways and means he could to procure my final destruction. For my mortal enemy has not only falsely surmised me to be a feigned person, giving me nicknames, so abusing the world, but also, to defer and put me from entry into England, has offered large sums of money to corrupt the princes and their ministers with whom I have been retained, and made importune labours to certain servants about my person to murder or poison me, and others to forsake and leave my righteous quarrel and to depart from my service, as Sir Robert Clifford and others. So that every man of reason may well perceive that Henry, calling himself King of England, needed not to have bestowed such great sums of treasure, nor so to have busied himself with importune and incessant labour and industry to compass my death and ruin, if I had been such a feigned person. But the truth of my cause being so manifest moved the most Christian King Charles, and the Lady Duchess Dowager of Burgundy, my most dear aunt, not only to acknowledge the truth thereof but lovingly to assist me.

'But it seems that God above, for the good of this whole island and the knitting of these two kingdoms of England and Scotland in a strait concord and amity by so great an obligation, has reserved the placing of me in the imperial throne of England for the arms and succours of your grace. Neither is it the first time that a king of Scotland has supported them that were reft and spoiled of the kingdom of England, as of late in fresh memory it was done in the person of Henry the Sixth. Wherefore, for that your grace has given clear signs that you are in no noble quality inferior to your royal ancestors, I, so distressed a prince, was hereby moved to come and put myself into your royal hands, desiring your assistance to recover my kingdom of England, promising faithfully to bear myself towards your grace no otherwise than if I were your own natural brother, and will, upon the recovery of mine inheritance, gratefully do to you all the pleasure that is in my utmost power.'

After Perkin had told his tale, King James answered bravely and wisely that, whosoever he were he should not repent him of putting himself into his hands. And from that time forth, though there wanted not some about him that would have persuaded him that all was but an illusion, yet notwithstanding, either taken by Perkin's amiable and alluring behaviour, or inclining to the recommendation of the great princes abroad, or willing to take an occasion of a war against King Henry, he entertained him in all things as became the person of Richard Duke of York, embraced his quarrel, and, the more to put it out of doubt that he took him to be a great prince and not a representation only, he gave consent that this Duke should take to wife the Lady Katherine Gordon daughter to the Earl of Huntley, being a near kinswoman to the King himself, and young virgin of excellent beauty and virtue.

Not long after, the King of Scots in person, with Perkin in his company, entered with a great army (though it consisted chiefly of borderers being raised somewhat suddenly) into Northumberland. And Perkin, for a perfume before him as he went, caused to be published a proclamation of this tenor following, in the name of Richard Duke of York, true inheritor of the crown of England:

It has pleased God, who puts down the mighty from their seat, and exalts the humble, and suffers not the hopes of the just to perish in the end, to give us means at the length to show ourselves armed unto our lieges and people of England. But far be it from us to intend their hurt or damage, or to make war upon them, otherwise than to deliver ourself and them from tyranny and oppression. For our mortal enemy Henry Tudor, a false usurper of the crown of England that to us by natural and lineal right appertains, knowing in his own heart our undoubted right (we being the very Richard Duke of York, younger son and now surviving heir-male of the noble and victorious

Edward the Fourth, late King of England), has not only deprived us of our kingdom but likewise by all foul and wicked means sought to betray us and bereave us of our life. Yet if his tyranny only extended itself to our person (although our royal blood teaches us to be sensible of injuries), it should be less to our grief. But this Tudor, who boasts himself to have overthrown a tyrant, has ever since his first entrance into his usurped reign put little in practice but tyranny and the feats thereof.

For King Richard, our unnatural uncle, although desire of rule did blind him yet in his other actions, like a true Plantagenet, was noble, and loved the honour of the realm and the contentment and comfort of his nobles and people. But this our mortal enemy, agreeable to the meanness of his birth, has trodden under foot the honour of this nation, selling our best confederates for money and making merchandise of the blood, estates and fortunes of our peers and subjects by feigned wars and dishonourable peace, only to enrich his coffers. Nor unlike has been his hateful misgovernment and evil deportments here at home. First he has, to fortify his false quarrel, caused divers nobles of this our realm (whom he held suspect and stood in dread of) to be cruelly murdered, as our cousin Sir William Stanley Lord Chamberlain, Sir Simon Mountfort, Sir Robert Ratcliffe, William Daubeney, Humphrey Stafford, and many others, besides such as have dearly bought their lives with intolerable ransoms, some of which nobles are now in the sanctuary. Also he has long kept, and yet keeps in prison our right entirely well-beloved cousin, Edward, son and heir to our uncle Duke of Clarence, and others, withholding from them their rightful inheritance, to the intent they should never be of might and power to aid and assist us at our need, after the duty of their legiances. He also married by compulsion certain of our sisters, and also the sister of our said cousin the Earl of Warwick, and divers other ladies of the royal blood, unto certain of his kinsmen and friends of simple and low degree, and, putting apart all well-disposed nobles, he has none in favour and trust about his person, but Bishop Fox, Smith, Bray, Lovel, Oliver King, David Owen, Riseley, Turbervile, Tyler, Cholmeley, Empson, James Hobarte, John Cutte, Garth, Henry

Wyate, and such other caitiffs and villains of birth, which by subtile inventions and pilling of the people have been the principal finders, occasioners, and counsellors of the misrule and mischief now reigning in England.

We remembering these premises, with the great and execrable offences daily committed and done by our foresaid great enemy and his adherents in breaking the liberties and franchises of our mother the holy church, upon pretences of wicked and heathenish policy, to the high displeasure of Almighty God; besides the manifold treasons, abominable murders, manslaughters, robberies, extortions, the daily pilling of the people by dismes, taskes, tallages, benevolences, and other unlawful impositions and grievous exactions, with many other heinous effects, to the likely destruction and desolation of the whole realm, shall by God's grace, and the help and assistance of the great lords of our blood, with the counsel of other sad persons, see that the commodities of our realm be employed to the most advantage of the same; the intercourse of merchandise betwixt realm and realm to be ministered and handled as shall more be to the common weal and prosperity of our subjects, and all such dismes, taskes, tallages, benevolences, unlawful impositions, and grievous exactions as be above rehearsed, to be foredone and laid apart, and never from henceforth to be called upon but in such cases as our noble progenitors kings of England have of old time been accustomed to have the aid, succour, and help of their subjects and true liegemen.

And further we do out of our grace and clemency hereby as well publish and promise to all our subjects remission and free pardon of all by-past offences whatsoever against our person or estate in adhering to our said enemy, by whom we know well they have been misled, if they shall within time convenient submit themselves unto us. And for such as shall come with the foremost to assist our righteous quarrel, we shall make them so far partakers of our princely favour and bounty as shall be highly for the comfort of them and theirs both during their life and after their death. As also we shall, by all means that God shall put into our hands, demean ourselves to give royal contentment to all degrees and estates of our people, maintaining the liberties of holy church in their entire, preserving the honours, privileges, and pre-eminences of our nobles from contempt or disparagement, according to the dignity of their blood. We shall also unyoke our people from all heavy burdens and endurances, and confirm our cities, boroughs, and towns in their charters and freedoms, with enlargement where it shall be deserved, and in all points give our subjects cause to think that the blessed and debonaire government of our noble father King Edward in his last times is in us revived.

And forasmuch as the putting to death or taking alive of our said mortal enemy may be a mean to stay much effusion of blood, which otherwise may ensue if by compulsion or fair promises he shall draw after him any number of our subjects to resist us, which we desire to avoid (though we be certainly informed that our said enemy is purposed and prepared to fly the land, having already made over great masses of the treasure of our crown the better to support him in foreign parts), we do hereby declare that whosoever shall take or distress our said enemy, though the party be of never so mean a condition, he shall be by us rewarded with £1,000 in money, forthwith to be laid down to him, and 100 marks by the year of inheritance, besides that he may otherwise merit, both toward God and all good people, for the destruction of such a tyrant.

Lastly, we do all men to wit[143] (and herein we take also God to witness) that whereas God has moved the heart of our dearest cousin the King of Scotland to aid us in person in this our righteous quarrel, that it is altogether without any pact or promise, or so much as demand of any thing that may prejudice our crown or subjects, but contrariwise with promise on our said cousin's part that, whensoever he shall find us in sufficient strength to get the upper hand of our enemy (which we hope will be very suddenly), he will forthwith peaceably return into his own kingdom, contenting himself only with the glory of so honourable an enterprise, and our true and faithful love and amity, which we shall ever by the grace of Almighty God so order as shall be to the great comfort of both kingdoms.

But Perkin's proclamation did little edify with the people of England. Neither was he the better welcome for the company he came in.

Wherefore the King of Scotland, seeing none came in to Perkin nor none stirred anywhere in his favour, turned his enterprise into a rode, and wasted and destroyed the country of Northumberland with fire and sword. But hearing that there were forces coming against him, and not willing that they should find his men heavy and laden with booty, he returned into Scotland with great spoils, deferring further prosecution till another time. It is said that Perkin, acting the part of a prince handsomely when he saw the Scottish fell to waste the country, came to the King in a passionate manner, making great lamentation, and desired that that might not be the manner of making the war, for that no crown was so dear to his mind as that he desired to purchase it with the blood and ruin of his country. Whereunto the King answered half in sport, that he doubted much he was careful for that that was none of his, and that he should be too good a steward for his enemy to save the country to his use.

By this time, being the eleventh year of the King, the interruption of trade between the English and the Flemish began to pinch the merchants of both nations very sore, which moved them by all means they could devise to affect and dispose their sovereigns respectively to open the intercourse again. Wherein time favoured them. For the Archduke[144] and his council began to see that Perkin would prove but a runagate and citizen of the world, and that it was the part of children to fall out about babies. And the King on his part, after the attempts upon Kent and Northumberland, began to have the business of Perkin in less estimation, so as he did not put it to account in any consultation of state. But that that moved him most was that, being a king that loved wealth and treasure, he could not endure to have trade sick, nor any obstruction to continue in the gate-vein that disperses that blood. And yet he kept state so far, as first to be sought unto. Wherein the Merchant Adventurers likewise, being a strong company at that time and well underset with rich men and good order, did hold out bravely, taking off the commodities of the kingdom, though they lay dead upon their hands for want of vent. At the last commissioners met at London to treat. On the King's part, Bishop Fox Lord Privy Seal, Viscount Wells, Kendall Prior of St John's, and Warham Master of the Rolls (who began to gain much upon the King's opinion), and Urswick, who was almost ever one, and Riseley. On the Archduke's part, the Lord Bevers his Admiral, the Lord Verunsell President of Flanders, and others. These concluded a perfect treaty both of amity and intercourse between the King and the Archduke, containing articles both of state, commerce, and free fishing.

This is that treaty that the Flemings call at this day *intercursus magnus*,[145] both because it is more complete than the precedent treaties of the third and fourth year of the King, and chiefly to give it a difference from the treaty that followed in the one and twentieth year of the King, which they call *intercursus malus*.[146] In this treaty there was an express article against the reception of the rebels of either prince by the other, purporting that if any such rebel should be required by the prince whose rebel he was of the prince confederate, that forthwith the prince confederate should by proclamation command him to avoid his country, which if he did not within fifteen days the rebel was to stand proscribed and put out of protection. But nevertheless in this article Perkin was not named, neither perhaps contained, because he was no rebel. But by this means his wings were clipped of his followers that were English. And it was expressly comprised in the treaty that it should extend to the territories of the Duchess Dowager. After the intercourse thus restored, the English merchants came again to their mansion at Antwerp, where they were received with procession and great joy.

The winter following, being the twelfth year of his reign, the King called again his parliament, where he did much exaggerate both the malice and the cruel predatory war lately made by the King of Scotland: that that King, being in amity with him, and no ways provoked, should so burn in hatred towards him as to drink of the lees and dregs of Perkin's intoxication, who was everywhere else detected and discarded, and that when he perceived it was out of his reach to do the King any hurt he had turned his arms upon unarmed and unprovided people, to spoil only and depopulate, contrary to the laws both of war and peace; concluding that he could neither with honour, nor with the safety of his people to whom he did owe protection, let pass these wrongs unrevenged. The parliament understood him well, and gave him a subsidy limited to the sum of 120,000 pounds, besides two fifteens: for his wars were always to him as a mine of treasure of a strange kind of ore, iron at the top, and gold and silver at the bottom.

At this parliament, for that there had been so much time spent in making laws the year before, and for that it was called purposely in respect of the Scottish war, there were no laws made to be remembered. Only there passed a law at the suit of the Merchant Adventurers of England against the Merchant Adventurers of London, for monopolising and exacting upon the trade, which it seems they did a little to save themselves after the hard time they had sustained by want of trade. But those innovations were taken away by parliament.

But it was fatal to the King to fight for his money. And though he avoided to fight with enemies abroad, yet he was still enforced to fight for it with rebels at home. For no sooner began the subsidy to be levied in Cornwall but the people there grew to grudge and murmur, the Cornish being a race of men stout of stomach, mighty of body and limb, and that lived hardly in a barren country, and many of them could for a need live underground, that were tinners. They muttered extremely that it was a thing not to be suffered that for a little stir of the Scots, soon blown over, they should be thus grinded to powder with payments, and said it was for them to pay that had too much, and lived idly, but they would eat their bread that they got with the sweat of their brows and no man should take it from them.

And as in the tides of people once up there want not commonly stirring winds to make them more rough, so this people did light upon two ringleaders or captains of the rout. The one was Michael Joseph, a blacksmith or farrier of Bodmin, a notable talking fellow, and no less desirous to be talked of. The other was Thomas Flammock, a lawyer, that by telling his neighbours commonly upon any occasion that the law was on their side had gotten great sway amongst them. This man talked learnedly, and as if he could tell how to make a rebellion and never break the peace. He told the people that subsidies were not to be granted nor levied in this case, that is for wars of Scotland, for that the law had provided another course, by service of escuage,[147] for those journeys; much less when all was quiet, and war was made but a pretence to poll and pill the people. And therefore that it was good they should not stand like a sheep before the shearers but put on harness and take weapons in their hands, yet to do no creature hurt, but go and deliver the King a strong petition for the laying down of those grievous payments and for the punishment of those that had given him that counsel, to make others beware how they did the like in time to come. And said for his part he did not see how they could do the duty of true Englishmen and good liegemen except they did deliver the King from such wicked ones that would destroy both him and the country. Their aim was at Archbishop Morton and Sir Reginald Bray, who were the King's screens in this envy.

After that these two, Flammock and the blacksmith, had by joint and several pratings[148] found tokens of consent in the multitude, they offered themselves to lead them until they should hear of better men to be their leaders, which they said would be ere long, telling them further that they would be but their servants, and first in every danger, but doubted not but to make both the west end and the east end of England to meet in so good a quarrel, and that all (rightly understood) was but for the King's service.

The people upon these seditious instigations did arm, most of them with bows and arrows, and bills, and such other weapons of rude and country people, and forthwith under the command of their leaders (which in such cases is ever at pleasure[149]) marched out of Cornwall through Devonshire unto Taunton in Somersetshire, without any slaughter, violence, or spoil of the country. At Taunton they killed in fury an officious and eager commissioner for the subsidy, whom they called the Provost of Perin. Thence they marched to Wells, where the Lord Audley (with whom their leaders had before some secret intelligence), a nobleman of an ancient family, but unquiet and popular[150] and aspiring to ruin, came in to them, and was by them with great gladness and cries of joy accepted as their general, they being now proud that they were led by a nobleman.

The Lord Audley led them on from Wells to Salisbury, and from Salisbury to Winchester. Thence the foolish people, who in effect led their leaders, had a mind to be led into Kent, fancying that the people there would join with them, contrary to all reason or judgement, considering the Kentish men had showed great loyalty and affection to the King so lately before. But the rude people had heard Flammock say that Kent was never conquered, and that they were the freest people of England. And upon these vain noises they looked for great matters at their hands, in a cause that they conceited to be for the liberty of the subject. But when they were come into Kent the country was so well settled, both by the King's late kind usage towards them and by the credit and power of the Earl of Kent, the Lord Abergavenny, and the Lord Cobham, as neither gentleman nor yeoman came in to their aid, which did much damp and dismay many of the simpler sort. Insomuch as divers of them did secretly fly from the army and went home; but the sturdier sort, and those that were most engaged, stood by it, and rather waxed proud than failed in hopes and courage. For as it did somewhat appal them that the people came not in to them, so it did no less encourage them that the King's forces had not set upon them, having marched from the west to the east of England. Wherefore they kept on their way and encamped upon Blackheath, between Greenwich and Eltham, threatening either to bid battle to the King (for now the seas went higher than to Morton and Bray), or to take London within his view, imagining with themselves there to find no less fear than wealth.

But to return to the King. When first he heard of this commotion of the Cornishmen occasioned by the subsidy, he was much troubled therewith: not for itself but in regard of the concurrence of other dangers that did hang over him at that time. For he doubted lest a war from Scotland, a rebellion from Cornwall, and the practices and conspiracies of Perkin and his partakers would come upon him at once, knowing well that it was a dangerous triplicity to a monarchy, to have the arms of a foreigner, the discontents of subjects, and the title of a pretender to meet. Nevertheless the occasion took him in some part well provided. For as soon as the parliament had broken up, the King had presently raised a puissant army to war upon Scotland. And King James of Scotland likewise on his part had made great preparations, either for defence or for a new assailing of England. But as for the King's forces, they were not only in preparation but in readiness presently to set forth, under the conduct of Daubeney the Lord Chamberlain. But as soon as the King understood of the rebellion of Cornwall, he stayed those forces, retaining them for his own service and safety. But therewithal he despatched the Earl of Surrey into the north, for the defence and strength of those parts in case the Scots should stir.

But for the course he held towards the rebels, it was utterly differing from his former custom and practice, which was ever full of forwardness and celerity to make head against them, or to set up them as soon as ever they were in action. This he was wont to do, but now, besides that he was attempered by years, and less in love with dangers by the continued fruition of a crown, it was a time when the various appearance to his thoughts of perils of several natures and from divers parts did make him judge it his best and surest way to keep his strength together in the seat and centre of his kingdom, according to the ancient Indian emblem – in such a swelling season, to hold the hand upon the middle of the bladder, that no side might rise.[151] Besides, there was no necessity put upon him to alter this counsel. For neither did the rebels spoil the country, in which case it had been dishonour to abandon his people, neither on the other side did their forces gather or increase, which might hasten him to precipitate, and assail them before they grew too strong. And lastly, both reason of estate and war seemed to agree with this course, for that insurrections of base people are commonly more furious in their beginnings. And by this means also he had them the more at vantage, being tired and harassed with a long march, and more at mercy, being cut off far from their country, and therefore not able by any sudden flight to get to retreat, and to renew the troubles.

When therefore the rebels were encamped in Blackheath upon the hill, whence they might behold the city of London and the fair valley about it, the King, knowing well that it stood him upon[152] by how much the more he had hitherto protracted the time in not encountering them, by so much the sooner to despatch with them, that it might appear to have been no coldness in fore-slowing but wisdom in choosing his time, resolved with all speed to assail them, and yet with that providence and surety as should leave little to venture or fortune. And having very great and puissant forces about him, the better to master all events and accidents he divided them into three parts. The first was led by the Earl of Oxford in chief, assisted by the Earls of Essex and Suffolk. These noblemen were appointed, with some corners of horse and bands of foot, and good store of artillery, wheeling about to put themselves beyond the hill where the rebels were encamped, and to beset all the skirts and descents thereof except those that lay towards London, thereby to have these wild beasts as it were in a toil. The second part of his forces (which were those that were to be most in action, and upon which he relied most for the fortune of the day) he did assign to be led by the Lord Chamberlain, who was appointed to set upon the rebels in front, from that side that is towards London. The third part of his forces (being likewise great and brave forces) he retained about himself, to be ready upon all events, to restore the fight or consummate the victory, and meanwhile to secure the city. And for that purpose he encamped in person in St George's Fields, putting himself between the city and the rebels.

But the city of London, especially at the first upon the near en-camping of the rebels, was in great tumult, as it uses to be[153] with wealthy and populous cities, especially those that, being for greatness and fortune queens of their regions, do seldom see out of their windows or from their towers an army of enemies. But that which troubled them most was the conceit that they dealt with a rout of people with whom there was no composition or condition,[154] orderly treating if need were, but likely to be bent altogether upon rapine and spoil. And although they had heard that the rebels had behaved themselves quietly and modestly by the way as they went, yet they doubted much that would not last, but rather make them more hungry and more in appetite to fall upon spoil in the end. Wherefore there was great running to and fro of people, some to the gates, some to the walls, some to the water side, giving themselves alarms and panic fears continually.

Nevertheless both Tate the Lord Mayor, and Shaw and Haddon the Sheriffs did their parts stoutly and well in arming and ordering the people, and the King likewise did adjoin some captains of experience in the wars to advise and assist the citizens. But soon after, when they understood that the King had so ordered the matter that the rebels must win three battles before they could approach the city, and that he had put his own person between the rebels and them, and that the great care was rather how to impound the rebels that none of them might escape than that any doubt was made to vanquish them, they grew to be quiet and out of fear, the rather for the confidence they reposed (which was not small) in the three leaders, Oxford, Essex, and Daubeney, all men well famed and loved amongst the people. As for Jasper Duke of Bedford, whom the King used to employ with the first in his wars, he was then sick and died soon after.

It was the two and twentieth of June, and a Saturday (which as the day of the week the King fancied), when the battle was fought, though the King had by all the art he could devise given out a false day, as if he prepared to give the rebels battle on the Monday following, the better to find them unprovided and in disarray. The lords that were appointed to circle the hill had some days before planted themselves as at the receipt,[155] in places convenient. In the afternoon towards the decline of the day (which was done the better to keep the rebels in opinion that they should not fight that day), the Lord Daubeney marched on towards them, and first beat some troops of them from Deptford Bridge, where they fought manfully, but being in no great number were soon driven back, and fled up to their main army upon the hill. The army at that time hearing of the approach of the King's forces, were putting themselves in array not without much confusion. But neither had they placed upon the first high ground towards the bridge any forces to second the troops below that kept the bridge, neither had they brought forwards their main battle (which stood in array far into the heath) near to the ascent of the hill, so that the Earl with his forces mounted the hill and recovered the plain without resistance. The Lord Daubeney charged them with great fury, inso-much as it had like by accident to have brandled the fortune of the day. For by inconsiderate forwardness in fighting in the head of his troops he was taken by the rebels, but immediately rescued and delivered. The rebels maintained the fight for a small time, and for their persons showed no want of courage. But being ill armed and ill led, and without horse or artillery, they were with no great difficulty cut in pieces and put to flight. And for their three leaders, the Lord Audley, the blacksmith, and Flammock, as commonly the captains of commotions are but half-couraged men, suffered themselves to be taken alive. The number slain on the rebels' part were some 2,000 men, their army amounting, as it is said, unto the number 16,000. The rest were in effect all taken, for that the hill (as was said) was encompassed with the King's forces round about. On the King's part there died about 300, most of them shot with arrows, which were reported to be of length of a tailor's yard,[156] so strong and mighty a bow the Cornishmen were said to draw.

The victory thus obtained the King created divers bannerets, as well upon Blackheath, where his lieutenant had won the field (whither he rode in person to perform the said creation), as in St George's Fields, where his own person had been encamped. And for matter of liberality, he did by open edict give the goods of all prisoners unto those that had taken them, either to take them in kind or compound for them as they could. After matter of honour and liberality followed matter of severity and execution. The Lord Audley was led from Newgate to Tower Hill in a paper coat painted with his own arms, the arms reversed, the coat torn, and at Tower Hill beheaded. Flammock and the blacksmith were hanged drawn and quartered at Tyburn, the blacksmith taking pleasure upon the hurdle[157] (as it seems by words that he uttered) to think that he should be famous in after-times. The King was once in mind to have sent down Flammock and the blacksmith to have been executed in Cornwall, for the more terror. But being advertised that the country was yet unquiet and boiling, he thought better not to irritate the people further. All the rest were pardoned by proclamation, and to take out their pardons under seal[158] as many as would. So that more than the blood drawn in the field, the King did satisfy himself with the lives of only three offenders for the expiation of this great rebellion.

It was a strange thing to observe the variety and inequality of the King's executions and pardons, and a man would think it at the first a kind of lottery or chance. But looking into it more nearly one shall find there was reason for it, much more perhaps than after so long a distance of time we can now discern. In the Kentish commotion (which was but a handful of men) there were executed to the number of 150, but in this so mighty a rebellion but three. Whether it were that the King put to account the men that were slain in the field, or that he was not willing to be severe in a popular cause, or that the harmless behaviour of this people, that came from the west of England to the east without mischief (almost) or spoil of the country, did somewhat mollify him and move him to compassion, or lastly, that he made a great difference between people that did rebel upon wantonness, and them that did rebel upon want.

After the Cornishmen were defeated there came from Calais to the King an honourable ambassage from the French King, which had arrived at Calais a month before, and was there stayed in respect of the troubles, but honourably entertained and defrayed. The King at their first coming sent unto them and prayed them to have patience till a little smoke that was raised in his country were over, which would soon be; slighting (as his manner was) that openly, which nevertheless he intended seriously.

This ambassage concerned no great affair, but only the prolongation of days for payment of money, and some other particular of the frontiers, and it was indeed but a wooing ambassage, with good respects to entertain the King in good affection. But nothing was done or handled to the derogation of the King's late treaty with the Italians.

But during the time that the Cornishmen were in their march towards London, the King of Scotland, well advertised of all that passed, and knowing himself sure of a war from England whensoever those stirs were appeased, neglected not his opportunity, but thinking the King had his hands full, entered the frontiers of England again with an army, and besieged the castle of Norham in person with part of his forces, sending the rest to forage the country. But Fox Bishop of Durham, a wise man and one that could see through the present to the future, doubting as much before, had caused his castle of Norham to be strongly fortified and furnished with all kind of munition, and had manned it likewise with a very great number of tall soldiers more than for the proportion of the castle, reckoning rather upon a sharp assault than a long siege. And for the country likewise, he had caused the people to withdraw their cattle and goods into fast places, that were not of easy approach, and sent in post to the Earl of Surrey (who was not far off in Yorkshire) to come in diligence to the succour. So the Scottish King both failed of doing good upon the castle, and his men had but a catching harvest of their spoils. And when he understood that the Earl of Surrey was coming on with great forces he returned back into Scotland. The Earl finding the castle freed, and the enemy retired, pursued with all celerity into Scotland, hoping to have overtaken the Scottish King, and to have given him battle. But not attaining him in time, sat down before the castle of Aton, one of the strongest places (then esteemed) between Berwick and Edinburgh, which in a small time he took. And soon after the Scottish King retiring further into his country, and the weather being extraordinary foul and stormy, the Earl returned into England. So that the expeditions on both parts were (in effect) but a castle taken and a castle distressed, not answerable to the puissance of the forces, nor to the heat of the quarrel, nor to the greatness of the expectation.

Amongst these troubles both civil and external came into England from Spain, Peter Hialas, some call him Elias (surely he was the forerunner of the good hap that we enjoy at this day: for his ambassage set the truce between England and Scotland, the truce drew on the peace, the peace the marriage, and the marriage the union of the kingdoms); a man of great wisdom and (as those times were) not unlearned, sent from Ferdinando and Isabella, Kings of Spain, unto the King to treat a marriage between Catherine, their second daughter, and Prince Arthur. This treaty was by him set in a very good way and almost brought to perfection. But it so fell out by the way that upon some conference that he had with the King touching this business, the King (who had a great dexterity in getting suddenly into the bosom of ambassadors of foreign princes, if he liked the men, insomuch as he would many times communicate with them of his own affairs, yea and employ them in his service), fell into speech and discourse incidently, concerning the ending of the debates and differences with Scotland. For the King naturally did not love the barren wars with Scotland, though he made his profit of the noise of them, and he wanted not in the council of Scotland those that would advise their King to meet him at the half way, and to give over the war with England, pretending to be good patriots but indeed favouring the affairs of the King. Only his heart was too great to begin with Scotland for the motion of peace.

On the other side he had met with an ally in Ferdinando of Aragon as fit for his turn as could be. For after that King Ferdinando had, upon assured confidence of the marriage to succeed, taken upon him the person of a fraternal ally to the King, he would not let, in a Spanish gravity, to counsel the King in his own affairs. And the King on his part, not being wanting to himself but making use of every man's humours, made his advantage of this in such things as he thought either not decent or not pleasant to proceed from himself, putting them off as done[159] by the counsel of Ferdinando. Wherefore he was content that Hialas, as in a matter moved and advised from Hialas himself, should go into Scotland to treat of a concord between the two kings. Hialas took it upon him, and coming to the Scottish King after he had with much art brought King James to hearken to the more safe and quiet counsels, wrote unto the King that he hoped that peace would with no great difficulty cement and close if he would send some wise and temperate counsellor of his own, that might treat of the conditions. Whereupon the King directed Bishop Fox (who at that time was at his castle of Norham) to confer with Hialas, and they both to treat with some commissioners deputed from the Scottish King.

The commissioners on both sides met. But after much dispute upon the articles and conditions of peace propounded upon either part they could not conclude a peace. The chief impediment thereof was the demand of the King to have Perkin delivered into his hands, as a reproach to all kings and a person not protected by the law of nations. The King of Scotland on the other side peremptorily denied so to do, saying that he for his part was no competent judge of Perkin's title, but that he had received him as a suppliant, protected him as a person fled for refuge, espoused him with his kinswoman and aided him with his arms, upon the belief that he was a prince, and therefore that he could not now with his honour so unrip and in a sort put a lie upon all that he had said and done before as to deliver him up to his enemies.

The Bishop likewise (who had certain proud instructions from the King, at the least in the front, though there were a pliant clause at the foot that remitted all to the Bishop's discretion, and required him by no means to break off in ill terms), after that he had failed to obtain the delivery of Perkin did move a second point of his instructions, which was that the Scottish King would give the King an interview in person at Newcastle. But this being reported to the Scottish King, his answer was that he meant to treat a peace and not to go a begging for it. The Bishop, also according to another article of his instructions, demanded restitution of the spoils taken by the Scottish or damages for the same. But the Scottish commissioners answered that that was but as water spilt upon the ground, which could not be gotten up again, and that the

King's people were better able to bear the loss than their master to repair it. But in the end, as persons capable of reason on both sides, they made rather a kind of recess than a breach of treaty, and concluded upon a truce for some months following.

But the King of Scotland, though he would not formally retract his judgement of Perkin, wherein he had engaged himself so far, yet in his private opinion, upon often speech with the Englishmen and divers other advertisements, began to suspect him for a counterfeit. Wherefore in a noble fashion he called him unto him, and recounted the benefits and favours that he had done him in making him his ally, and in provoking a mighty and opulent King by an offensive war in his quarrel, for the space of two years together; nay more, that he had refused an honourable peace, whereof he had a fair offer if he would have delivered him, and that to keep his promise with him he had deeply offended both his nobles and people, whom he might not hold in any long discontent; and therefore required him to think of his own fortunes, and to choose out some fitter place for his exile, telling him withal that he could not say but the English had forsaken him before the Scottish, for that upon two several trials none had declared themselves on his side. But nevertheless he would make good what he said to him at his first receiving, which was that he should not repent him for putting himself into his hands, for that he would not cast him off, but help him with shipping and means to transport him where he should desire.

Perkin, not descending at all from his stagelike greatness, answered the King in few words that he saw his time was not yet come, but whatsoever his fortunes were he should both think and speak honour of the King. Taking his leave, he would not think on Flanders, doubting it was but hollow ground for him since the treaty of the Archduke concluded the year before, but took his lady, and such followers as would not leave him, and sailed over into Ireland.

This twelfth year of the King, a little before this time, Pope Alexander, who loved best those princes that were furthest off and with whom he had least to do, and taking very thankfully the King's late entrance into league for the defence of Italy, did remunerate him with a hallowed sword and cap of maintenance,[160] sent by his nuncio. Pope Innocent had done the like, but it was not received in that glory. For the

King appointed the Mayor and his brethren to meet the Pope's orator at London Bridge, and all the streets between the bridge foot and the palace of Paul's (where the King then lay) were garnished with the citizens, standing in their liveries. And the morrow after, being Allhallows-day, the King attended with many of his prelates and nobles and principal courtiers, went in procession to Paul's, and the cap and sword were borne before him. And after the procession, the King himself remaining seated in the quire, the Lord Archbishop upon the greese of the quire made a long oration setting forth the greatness and eminency of that honour that the Pope (in these ornaments and ensigns of benediction) had done the King, and how rarely and upon what high deserts they used to be bestowed, and then recited the King's principal acts and merits, which had made him appear worthy in the eyes of his Holiness of this great honour.

All this while the rebellion of Cornwall (whereof we have spoken) seemed to have no relation to Perkin, save that perhaps Perkin's proclamation had stricken upon the right vein in promising to lay down exactions and payments, and so had made them now and then have a kind thought on Perkin. But now these bubbles by much stirring began to meet, as they use to do upon the top of water. The King's lenity (by that time the Cornish rebels who were taken and pardoned, and as it was said many of them sold by them that had taken them for twelve pence and two shillings apiece, were come down into their country) had rather emboldened them than reclaimed them. Insomuch as they stuck not to say to their neighbours and countrymen that the King did well to pardon them, for that he knew he should leave few subjects in England if he hanged all that were of their mind, and began whetting and inciting one another to renew the commotion. Some of the subtlest of them, hearing of Perkin's being in Ireland, found means to send to him to let him know that if he would come over to them they would serve him.

When Perkin heard this news he began to take heart again, and advised upon it with his council, which were principally three: Herne a mercer that had fled for debt, Skelton a tailor, and Astley a scrivener (for secretary Fryon was gone). These told him that he was mightily overseen, both when he went into Kent and when he went into

Scotland, the one being a place so near London, and under the King's nose, and the other a nation so distasted with the people of England that if they had loved him never so well yet they would never have taken his part in that company. But if he had been so happy as to have been in Cornwall at the first, when the people began to take arms there, he had been crowned at Westminster before this time. For these kings (as he had now experience) would sell poor princes for shoes, but he must rely wholly upon people, and therefore advised him to sail over with all possible speed into Cornwall, which accordingly he did, having in his company four small barks with some sixscore or sevenscore fighting men. He arrived in September at Whitsand Bay and forthwith came to Bodmin, the blacksmith's town, where there assembled unto him to the number of 3,000 men of the rude people.

There he set forth a new proclamation, stroking the people with fair promises and humouring them with invectives against the King and his government. And as it fares with smoke that never leeses itself till it be at the highest, he did now before his end raise his style, entitling himself no more Richard Duke of York but Richard the Fourth, King of England. His council advised him by all means to make himself master of some good walled town, as well to make his men find the sweetness of rich spoils, and to allure to him all loose and lost people by like hopes of booty, as to be a sure retreat to his forces in case they should have any ill day or unlucky chance in the field. Wherefore they took heart to them, and went on and besieged the city of Exeter, the principal town for strength and wealth in those parts.

When they were come before Exeter they forbore to use any force at the first but made continual shouts and outcries to terrify the inhabitants, and did likewise in divers places call and talk to them from under the walls, to join with them and be of their party, telling them that the King[161] would make them another London if they would be the first town that should acknowledge him. But they had not the wit to send to them, in any orderly fashion, agents or chosen men to tempt them and to treat with them. The citizens on their part showed themselves stout and loyal subjects; neither was here so much as any tumult or division amongst them, but all prepared themselves for a valiant defence and making good the town. For well they saw that the rebels were of no such number or power that they needed to fear them as yet, and well they hoped that before their numbers increased the King's succours would come in. And howsoever, they thought it the extremest of evils to put themselves at the mercy of those hungry and disorderly people. Wherefore, setting all things in good order within the town, they nevertheless let down with cords from several parts of the walls privily several messengers (that if one came to mischance another might pass on), which should advertise the King of the state of the town and implore his aid.

Perkin also doubted that succours would come ere long and therefore resolved to use his utmost force to assault the town. And for that purpose having mounted scaling ladders in divers places upon the walls, made at the same instant an attempt to force one of the gates. But having no artillery nor engines, and finding that he could do no good by ramming with logs of timber, nor by the use of iron bars and iron crows and such other means at hand, he had no way left him but to set one of the gates on fire, which he did. But the citizens well perceiving the danger before the gate could be fully consumed, blocked up the gate and some space about it on the inside with faggots and other fuel, which they likewise set on fire and so repulsed fire with fire, and in the meantime raised up rampiers of earth, and cast up deep trenches to serve instead of wall and gate. And for the escalades,[162] they had so bad success as the rebels were driven from the walls with the loss of 200 men.

The King when he heard of Perkin's siege of Exeter, made sport with it, and said to them that were about him that the King of rake-hells was landed in the west, and that he hoped now to have the honour to see him, which he could never yet do. And it appeared plainly to those that were about the King that he was indeed much joyed with the news of Perkin's being in English ground, where he could have no retreat by land, thinking now that he should be cured of those privy stitches that he had had long about his heart, and had sometimes broken his sleep in the midst of all his felicity. And to set all men's hearts on fire, he did by all possible means let it appear that those that should now do him service to make an end of these troubles should be no less accepted of him than he that came upon the eleventh hour and had the whole wages of the day.[163]

Therefore now, like the end of a play a great number came upon the stage at once. He sent the Lord Chamberlain, and the Lord Brooke, and Sir Rice ap Thomas, with expedite forces to speed to Exeter to the rescue of the town, and to spread the fame of his own following in person with a royal army. The Earl of Devonshire and his son, with the Carews and the Fulfordes and other principal persons of Devonshire (uncalled from the court, but hearing that the King's heart was so much bent upon this service), made haste with troops that they had raised to be the first that should succour the city of Exeter and prevent the King's succours. The Duke of Buckingham likewise with many brave gentlemen put themselves in arms, not staying either the King's or Lord Chamberlain's coming on, but making a body of forces of themselves the more to endear their merit, signifying to the King their readiness, and desiring to know his pleasure. So that according to the proverb, in the coming down every saint did help.

Perkin, hearing this thunder of arms and preparations against him from so many parts, raised his siege and marched to Taunton, beginning already to squint one eye upon the crown and another upon the sanctuary, though the Cornishmen were become like metal often fired and quenched, churlish, and that would sooner break than bow, swearing and vowing not to leave him till the uttermost drop of their blood were spilt. He was at his rising from Exeter between six and seven thousand strong, many having come unto him after he was set before Exeter, upon fame of so great enterprise and to partake of the spoil, though upon the raising of the siege some did slip away. When he was come near Taunton he dissembled all fear, and seemed all the day to use diligence in preparing all things ready to fight. But about midnight he fled with threescore horse to Beaulieu in the New Forest, where he and divers of his company registered themselves sanctuary men, leaving his Cornishmen to the four winds, but yet thereby easing them of their vow, and using his wonted compassion, not to be by when his subjects' blood should be spilt. The King as soon as he heard of Perkin's flight, sent presently 500 horse to pursue and apprehend him before he should get either to the sea or to that same little island called a sanctuary. But they came too late for the latter of these. Therefore all they could do was to beset the sanctuary, and to maintain a strong watch about it, till the King's pleasure were further known.

As for the rest of the rebels, they (being destituted of their head) without stroke stricken submitted themselves unto the King's mercy. And the King, who commonly drew blood (as physicians do) rather to save life than to spill it, and was never cruel when he was secure, now he saw the danger was past, pardoned them all in the end, except some few desperate persons that he reserved to be executed, the better to set off his mercy towards the rest. There were also sent with all speed some horse to St Michael's Mount in Cornwall, where the Lady Katherine Gordon was left by her husband, whom in all fortunes she entirely loved, adding the virtues of a wife to the virtues of her sex. The King sent in the greater diligence, not knowing whether she might be with child, whereby the business would not have ended in Perkin's person. When she was brought to the King it was commonly said that the King received her not only with compassion but with affection, pity giving more impression to her excellent beauty. Wherefore comforting her, to serve as well his eye as his fame, he sent her to his queen to remain with her, giving her very honourable allowance for the support of her estate, which she enjoyed both during the King's life and many years after. The name of the White Rose that had been given to her husband's false title, was continued in common speech to her true beauty.

The King went forwards on his journey and made a joyful entrance into Exeter, where he gave the citizens great commendations and thanks, and taking the sword he wore from his side, he gave it to the Mayor and commanded it should be ever after carried before him. There also he caused to be executed some of the ringleaders of the Cornishmen, in sacrifice to the citizens whom they had put in fear and trouble. At Exeter the King consulted with his council whether he should offer life to Perkin if he would quit the sanctuary and voluntarily submit himself. The council were divided in opinion. Some advised the King to take him out of sanctuary perforce and to put him to death, as in a case of necessity, which in itself dispenses with consecrated places and things, wherein they doubted not also but the King should find the Pope tractable to ratify his deed either by declaration or at least by indulgence. Others were of opinion, since all was now safe and no further hurt could be done, that it was not worth the exposing of the King to new scandal and envy. A third sort fell upon the opinion that it was not possible for the King ever either to satisfy the world well touching the imposture, or to learn out the bottom of the conspiracy, except by promise of life and pardon and other fair mean he should get Perkin into his hands.

But they did all in their preambles much bemoan the King's case with a kind of indignation at his fortune, that a prince of his high wisdom and virtue should have been so long and so oft exercised and vexed with idols. But the King said that it was the vexation of God Almighty himself to be vexed with idols, and therefore that that was not to trouble any of his friends, and that for himself he always despised them, but was grieved that they had put his people to such trouble and misery. But in conclusion he leaned to the third opinion, and so sent some to deal with Perkin, who seeing himself a prisoner and destitute of all hopes, having tried princes and people great and small, and found all either false, faint or unfortunate, did gladly accept of the condition. The King did also while he was at Exeter appoint the Lord Darcy and others commissioners for the fining of all such as were of any value, and had any hand or partaking in the aid or comfort of Perkin or the Cornishmen, either in the field or in the flight. These commissioners proceeded with such strictness and severity as did much obscure the King's mercy in sparing of blood, with the bleeding of so much treasure.

Perkin was brought unto the King's court, but not to the King's presence, though the King to satisfy his curiosity saw him sometimes out of a window or in passage. He was in show at liberty, but guarded with all care and watch that was possible, and willed to follow the King to London. But from his first appearance upon the stage in his new person of a sycophant or juggler, instead of his former person of a prince, all men may think how he was exposed to the derision not only of the courtiers but also of the people, who flocked about him as he went along, that one might know afar off where the owl was by the flight of birds, some mocking, some wondering, some cursing, some prying and picking matter out of his countenance and gesture to talk of. So that the false honour and respects that he had so long enjoyed was plentifully repaid in scorn and contempt.

As soon as he was come to London the King gave also the city the solace of this may-game. For he was conveyed leisurely on horseback, but not in any ignominious fashion, through Cheapside and Cornhill to the Tower, and from thence back again unto Westminster with the churmne of a thousand taunts and reproaches. But to amend the show, there followed a little distance off Perkin, an inward counsellor of his, one that had been serjeant farrier to the King. This fellow, when Perkin took sanctuary, chose rather to take a holy habit than a holy place, and clad himself like a hermit, and in that weed wandered about the country till he was discovered and taken. But this man was bound hand and foot upon the horse, and came not back with Perkin but was left at the Tower, and within few days after executed.

Soon after, now that Perkin could tell better what himself was, he was diligently examined, and after his confession taken, an extract was made of such parts of them as were thought fit to be divulged, which was printed and dispersed abroad. Wherein the King did himself no right, for as there was a laboured tale of particulars of Perkin's father and mother and grandsire and grandmother and uncles and cousins, by names and surnames, and from what places he travelled up and down, so there was little or nothing to purpose of anything concerning his designs or any practices that had been held with him, nor the Duchess of Burgundy herself, that all the world did take knowledge of as the person that had put life and being into the whole business, so much as named or pointed at. So that men missing of that they looked for, looked about for they knew not what, and were in more doubt than before. But the King chose rather not to satisfy than to kindle coals. At that time also it did not appear by any new examinations or commitment that any other person of quality was discovered or appeached, though the King's closeness made that a doubt dormant.

About this time a great fire in the night-time suddenly began at the King's palace of Sheen, near unto the King's own lodgings, whereby a great part of the building was consumed, with much costly household stuff, which gave the King occasion of building from the ground that fine pile of Richmond, which is standing.

Somewhat before this time also, there fell out a memorable accident. There was one Sebastian Cabot,[164] a Venetian, dwelling in Bristol, a man seen and expert in cosmography and navigation. This man, seeing the success and emulating perhaps the enterprise of Christopherus Columbus in that fortunate discovery towards the southwest that had been by him made some six years before, conceited with himself that lands might likewise be discovered towards the northwest. And surely, it may be he had more firm and pregnant conjectures of it than Columbus had of his at the first. For the two great islands of the old and new world, being in the shape and making of them broad towards the north and pointed towards the south, it is likely that the discovery first began where the lands did nearest meet. And there had been before that time a discovery of some lands that they took to be islands, and were indeed the continent of America, towards the northwest. And it may be that some relation of this nature, coming afterwards to the knowledge of Columbus and by him suppressed (desirous rather to make his enterprise the child of science and fortune, than the follower of a former discovery), did give him better assurance that all was not sea from the west of Europe and Africa unto Asia than either Seneca's prophecy, or Plato's antiquities, or the nature of the tides and land winds and the like, which were the conjectures that were given out whereupon he should have relied, though I am not ignorant that it was likewise laid unto the casual and wind-beaten discovery a little before of a Spanish pilot who died in the house of Columbus. But this Cabot, bearing the King in hand that he would find out an island endued with rich commodities, procured him to man and victual a ship at Bristol for the discovery of that island, with whom ventured also three small ships of London merchants, fraught with some gross and slight wares, fit for commerce with barbarous people.

He sailed, as he affirmed at his return (and made a card thereof), very far westwards, with a quarter of the north on the north side of Terra de Labrador, until he came to the latitude of sixty-seven degrees and a half, finding the seas still open. It is certain also that the King's fortune had a tender of that great empire of the West Indies. Neither was it a refusal on the King's part, but a delay by accident that put by so great an acquest. For Christopherus Columbus, refused by the King of Portugal (who would not embrace at once both east and west), employed his brother Bartholomeus Columbus unto King Henry to negotiate for his discovery. And it so fortuned that he was taken by pirates at sea, by which accidental impediment he was long ere he came to the King; so long, that before he had obtained a capitulation with the King for his brother the enterprise by him was achieved, and so the West Indies by providence were then reserved for the crown of Castilia. Yet this sharpened the King so that not only in this voyage, but again in the sixteenth year of his reign, and likewise in the eighteenth thereof, he granted forth new commissions for the discovery and investing of unknown lands.

In his fourteenth year also, by God's wonderful providence, that bows things unto his will, and hangs great weights upon small wires, there fell out a trifling and untoward accident that drew on great and happy effects. During the truce with Scotland there were certain Scottish young gentlemen that came into Norham town, and there made merry with some of the English of the town, and having little to do, went sometimes forth and would stand looking upon the castle. Some of the garrison of the castle, observing this their doing twice or thrice, and having not their minds purged of the late ill blood of hostility, either suspected them or quarrelled them for spies. Whereupon they fell at ill words, and from words to blows, so that many were wounded of either side, and the Scottishmen, being strangers in the town, had the worst, insomuch that some of them were slain and the rest made haste home. The matter being complained on and often debated before the wardens of marches of both sides, and no good order taken, the King of Scotland took it to himself, and being much kindled, sent a herald to the King to make protestation that if reparation were not done according to the conditions of the truce his King did denounce war. The King, who had often tried fortune and was inclined to peace, made answer that what had been done was utterly against his will and without his privity, but if the garrison soldiers had been in fault he would see them punished, and the truce in all points to be preserved. But this answer seemed to the Scottish King but a delay to make the complaint breathe out with time and therefore it did rather exasperate him than satisfy him. Bishop Fox, understanding from the King that the Scottish King was still discontent and impatient, being troubled that the occasion of breaking the truce should grow from his men, sent many humble and deprecatory letters to the Scottish King to appease him. Whereupon King James, mollified by the Bishop's submiss and eloquent letters, wrote back unto him that though he were in part moved by his letters yet he should not be fully satisfied except he spoke with him, as well about the compounding of the present differences as about other matters that might concern the good of both kingdoms.

The Bishop, advising first with the King, took his journey for Scotland. The meeting was at Melrose, an abbey of the Cistercians where the King then abode. The King first roundly uttered unto the Bishop his offence conceived for the insolent breach of truce by his men of Norham castle, whereunto Bishop Fox made such a humble and smooth answer as it was like oil into the wound, whereby it began to heal. And this was done in the presence of the King and his council. After the King spoke with the Bishop apart and opened himself unto him, saying that these temporary truces and peaces were soon made and soon broken, but that he desired a straiter amity with the King of England; discovering his mind, that if the King would give him in marriage the Lady Margaret, his eldest daughter, that indeed might be a knot indissoluble; that he knew well what place and authority the Bishop deservedly had with his master; therefore if he would take the business to heart and deal in it effectually, he doubted not but it would succeed well. The Bishop answered soberly that he thought himself rather happy than worthy to be an instrument in such a matter, but would do his best endeavour. Wherefore the Bishop returning to the King and giving him account of what had passed, and finding the King more than well disposed in it, gave the King advice first to proceed to conclusion of peace, and then to go on with the treaty of marriage by degrees. Hereupon a peace was concluded, which was published a little before Christmas in the fourteenth year of the King's reign, to continue for both the kings' lives and the over-liver of them and a year after. In this peace there was an article contained that no Englishman should enter into Scotland, and no Scottishman into England, without letters commendatory from the kings of either nation. This at the first sight might seem a means to continue a strangeness between the nations, but it was done to lock in the borderers.

This year there was also born to the King a third son, who was christened by the name of Edmond, and shortly after died. And much about the same time came news of the death of Charles the French King, for whom there were celebrated solemn and princely obsequies.

It was not long but Perkin, who was made of quicksilver (which is hard to hold or imprison) began to stir. For deceiving his keepers, he took him to his heels and made speed to the sea coast. But presently all corners were laid for him, and such diligent pursuit and search made as he was fain to turn back and get him to the house of Bethlehem, called the Priory of Sheen (which had the privilege of sanctuary), and put himself into the hands of the Prior of that monastery. The Prior was thought a holy man, and much reverenced in those days. He came to the King and besought the King for Perkin's life only, leaving him otherwise to the King's discretions. Many about the King were again more hot than ever to have the King to take him forth and hang him. But the King, that had a high stomach and could not hate any that he despised, bid take him forth and set the knave in the stocks. And so promising the Prior his life, he caused him to be brought forth. And within two or three days after, upon a scaffold set up in the palace court at Westminster, he was fettered and set in the stocks for the whole day. And the next day after the like was done by him at the cross in Cheapside, and in both places he read his confession of which we made mention before, and was from Cheapside conveyed and laid up in the Tower. Notwithstanding all this, the King was (as was partly touched before) grown to be such a partner with fortune as nobody could tell what actions the one and what the other owned. For it was believed generally that Perkin was betrayed, and that this escape was not without the King's privity, who had him all the time of his flight in a line, and that the King did this to pick a quarrel to him, to put him to death, and to be rid of him at once, which is not probable, for that the same instruments who observed him in his flight might have kept him from getting into sanctuary.

But it was ordained that this winding-ivy of a Plantagenet should kill the true tree itself. For Perkin, after he had been a while in the Tower, began to insinuate himself into the favour and kindness of his keepers, servants to the Lieutenant of the Tower, Sir John Digby, being four in number: Strangeways, Blewet, Astwood, and Long-Roger. These varlets with mountains of promises he sought to corrupt, to obtain his escape. But knowing well that his own fortunes were made so contemptible as he could feed no man's hopes, and by hopes he must work for rewards he had none, he had contrived with himself a vast and tragical plot, which was to draw to his company Edward Plantagenet Earl of Warwick,[165] then prisoner in the Tower, whom the weary life of a long imprisonment and the often and renewing fears of being put to death had softened to take any impression of counsel for his liberty. This young prince he thought these servants would look upon, though not upon himself. And therefore, after that by some message by one or two of them he had tasted of the Earl's consent, it was agreed that these four should murder their master the Lieutenant secretly in the night, and make their best of such money and portable goods of his as they should find ready at hand, and get the keys of the Tower, and presently let forth Perkin and the Earl. But this conspiracy was revealed in time before it could be executed. And in this again the opinion of the King's great wisdom did surcharge him with a sinister fame, that Perkin was but his bait to entrap the Earl of Warwick.

And in the very instant while this conspiracy was in working (as if that also had been the King's industry) it was fatal that there should break forth a counterfeit earl of Warwick, a cordwainer's son, whose name was Ralph Wilford, a young man taught and set on by an Augustinian friar called Patrick. They both from the parts of Suffolk came forwards into Kent, where they did not only privily and underhand give out that this Wilford was the true Earl of Warwick, but also the friar, finding some light credence in the people, took the boldness in the pulpit to declare as much and to incite the people to come in to his aid. Whereupon they were both presently apprehended and the young fellow executed, and the friar condemned to perpetual imprisonment. This also happening so opportunely to represent the danger to the King's estate from the Earl of Warwick, and thereby to colour the King's severity that followed, together with the madness of the friar, so vainly and desperately to divulge a treason before it had gotten any manner of strength, and the saving of the friar's life, which nevertheless was indeed but the privilege of his order,[166] and the pity in the common people (which if it run in a strong stream does ever cast up scandal and envy), made it generally rather talked than believed that all was but the King's device. But howsoever it were, hereupon Perkin (that had offended against grace now the third time) was at the last proceeded with, and by commissioners of Oyer and Determiner[167] arraigned at Westminster, upon divers treasons committed and perpetrated after his coming on land within this kingdom (for so the judges advised, for that he was a foreigner), and condemned, and a few days after executed at Tyburn, where he did again openly read his confession and take it upon his death to be true. This was the end of this little cockatrice of a king, that was able to destroy those that did not espy him first. It was one of the longest plays of that kind that has been in memory, and might perhaps have had another end, if he had not met with a king both wise, stout, and fortunate.

As for Perkin's three counsellors, they had registered themselves sanctuary men when their master did, and whether upon pardon obtained or continuance within the privilege, they came not to be proceeded with.

There was executed with Perkin the Mayor of Cork and his son, who had been principal abettors of his treasons. And soon after were likewise condemned eight other persons about the Tower conspiracy, whereof four were the Lieutenant's men. But of those eight but two were executed. And immediately after was arraigned before the Earl of Oxford (then for the time High Steward England) the poor prince, the Earl of Warwick; not for the attempt to escape simply, for that was not acted (and besides, the imprisonment not being for treason, the escape by law could not be treason), but for conspiring with Perkin to raise sedition and to destroy the King. And the Earl confessing the indictment had judgement, and was shortly after beheaded on Tower Hill.

This was also the end not only of this noble and commiserable person Edward the Earl of Warwick, eldest son to the Duke of Clarence, but likewise of the line-male of the Plantagenets, which had flourished in great royalty and renown from the time of the famous king of England, King Henry the Second. Howbeit it was a race often dipped in their own blood, it has remained since, only transplanted into other names, as well of the imperial line as of other noble houses. But it was neither guilt of crime, nor reason of state, that could quench the envy that was upon the King for this execution. So that he thought good to export it out of the land, and to lay it upon his new ally Ferdinando King of Spain. For these two kings understanding one another at half a word, so it was that there were letters showed out of Spain, whereby in the passages concerning the treaty of the marriage, Ferdinando had written to the King in plain terms that he saw no assurance of his succession as long as the Earl of Warwick lived, and that he was loath to send his daughter to troubles and dangers. But hereby as the King did in some part remove the envy from himself, so he did not observe that he did withal bring a kind of malediction and infausting upon the marriage, as an ill prognostic, which in event so far proved true, as both Prince Arthur enjoyed a very small time after the marriage, and the Lady Catherine herself (a sad and a religious woman) long after, when King Henry the Eighth his resolution of a divorce from her was first made known to her, used some words that she had not offended but it was a judgement of God, for that her former marriage was made in blood, meaning that of the Earl of Warwick.

This fifteenth year of the King there was a great plague both in London and in divers parts of the kingdom. Wherefore the King, after often change of places, whether to avoid the danger of the sickness or to give occasion of an interview with the Archduke, or both, sailed over with his queen to Calais. Upon his coming thither the Archduke sent an honourable ambassage unto him, as well to welcome him into those parts as to let him know that if it pleased him he would come and do him reverence. But it was said withal, that the King might be pleased to appoint some place that were out of any walled town or fortress, for that he had denied the same upon like occasion to the French King. And though he said he made a great difference between the two kings, yet he would be loath to give a precedent that might make it after to be expected at his hands by another whom he trusted less. The King accepted of the courtesy and admitted of his excuse, and appointed the place to be at St Peter's Church without Calais. But withal he did visit the Archduke with ambassadors sent from himself, which were the Lord St John and the secretary, unto whom the Archduke did the honour as (going to mass at St Omer's) to set the Lord St John on his right hand and the secretary on his left, and so to ride between them to church.

The day appointed for the interview the King went on horseback some distance from St Peter's Church to receive the Archduke. And upon their approaching the Archduke made haste to light and offered to hold the King's stirrup at his alighting, which he would not permit, but descending from horseback they embraced with great affection. And withdrawing into the church to a place prepared they had long conference, not only upon the confirmation of former treaties and the freeing of commerce, but upon cross-marriages to be had between the Duke of York,[168] the King's second son, and the Archduke's daughter; and again between Charles, the Archduke's son and heir, and Mary, the King's second daughter. But these blossoms of unripe marriages were but of friendly wishes, and the airs of loving entertainment, though one of them[169] came afterwards to a conclusion in treaty, though not in effect.

But during the time that the two princes conversed and communed together in the suburbs of Calais, the demonstrations on both sides were passing hearty and affectionate, especially on the part of the Archduke, who (besides that he was a prince of an excellent good nature) being conscious to himself how drily the King had been used by his council in the matter of Perkin, did strive by all means to recover it in the King's affection. And having also his ears continually beaten with the counsels of his father and father-in-law, who in respect of their jealous hatred against the French King did always advise the Archduke to anchor himself upon the amity of King Henry of England, was glad upon this occasion to put in ure and practice their precepts, calling the King patron, and father, and protector (these very words the King repeats, when he certified of the loving behaviour of the Archduke to the city), and what else he could devise to express his love and observance to the King. There came also to the King the Governor of Picardy and the Bailiff of Amiens, sent from Lewis the French King[170] to do him honour, and to give him knowledge of his victory and winning of the duchy of Milan.[171] It seems the King was well pleased with the honours he received from those parts while he was at Calais, for he did himself certify all the news and occurrents of them in every particular from Calais to the Mayor and Aldermen of London, which no doubt made no small talk in the city. For the King, though he could not entertain the goodwill of the citizens as Edward the Fourth did, yet by affability and other princely graces did ever make very much of them, and apply himself to them.

This year also died John Morton, Archbishop of Canterbury, Chancellor of England, and cardinal. He was a wise man and an eloquent, but in his nature harsh and haughty, much accepted by the King but envied by the nobility and hated of the people. Neither was his name left out of Perkin's proclamation for any good will, but they would not bring him in amongst the King's casting-counters because he had the image and superscription upon him of the Pope, in his honour of cardinal. He won the King with secrecy and diligence, but chiefly because he was his old servant in his less fortunes, and also for that in his affections he was not without an inveterate malice against the house of York, under whom he had been in trouble. He was willing also to take envy from the King more than the King was willing to put upon him. For the King cared not for subterfuges, but would stand envy, and appear in any thing that was to his mind, which made envy still grow upon him, more universal, but less daring. But in the matter of exactions time did after show that the Bishop in feeding the King's humour did rather temper it. He had been by Richard the Third committed as in custody to the Duke of Buckingham, whom he did secretly incite to revolt from King Richard. But after the Duke was engaged, and thought the Bishop should have been his chief pilot in the tempest, the Bishop was gotten into the cock-boat and fled over beyond seas. But whatsoever else was in the man he deserves a most happy memory, in that he was the principal means of joining the two Roses. He died of great years, but of strong health and powers.

The next year, which was the sixteenth year of the King and the year of our Lord one thousand five hundred, was the year of jubilee at Rome. But Pope Alexander, to save the hazard and charges of men's journeys to Rome, thought good to make over those graces by exchange to such as would pay a convenient rate, seeing they could not come to fetch them. For which purpose was sent into England Gasper Pons, a Spaniard, the Pope's commissioner, better chosen than were the commissioners of Pope Leo afterwards employed for Germany, for he carried the business with great wisdom and semblance of holiness, insomuch as he levied great sums of money within this land to the Pope's use, with little or no scandal. It was thought the King shared in the money, but it appears by a letter that Cardinal Adrian, the King's pensioner, wrote to the King from Rome some few years after, that this was not so. For this cardinal, being to persuade Pope Julius on the King's behalf to expedite the bull of dispensation for the marriage between Prince Henry and the Lady Catherine, finding the Pope difficile in granting thereof, does use it as a principal argument concerning the King's merit towards that see[172] that he had touched none of those deniers[173] that had been levied by Pons in England. But that it might the better appear (for the satisfaction of the common people) that this was consecrate money, the same nuncio brought unto the King a brief from the Pope, wherein the King was exhorted and summoned to come in person against the Turk. For that the Pope, out of the care of a universal father, seeing almost under his eyes the successes and progresses of that great enemy of the faith, had had in the conclave, and with the assistance of the ambassadors of foreign princes, divers consultations about a holy war and general expedition of Christian princes against the Turk. Wherein it was agreed and thought fit that the Hungarians, Polonians, and Bohemians should make a war upon Thracia; the French and Spaniards upon Graecia; and that the Pope (willing to sacrifice himself in so good a cause) in person, and in company of the King of England, the Venetians (and such other states as were great in maritime power), would sail with a puissant navy through the Mediterranean unto Constantinople. And that to this end his Holiness had sent nuncios to all Christian princes, as well for a cessation of all quarrels and differences amongst themselves as for speedy preparations and contributions of forces and treasure for this sacred enterprise.

To this the King (who understood well the court of Rome) made an answer rather solemn than serious, signifying, 'That no prince on earth should be more forward and obedient both by his person and by all his possible forces and fortunes to enter into this sacred war than himself.

But that the distance of place was such, as no forces that he should raise for the seas could be levied or prepared but with double the charge and double the time (at the least) that they might be from the other princes that had their territories nearer adjoining. Besides, that neither the manner of his ships (having no galleys) nor the experience of his pilots and mariners could be so apt for those seas as theirs. And therefore that his Holiness might do well to move one of those other kings, who lay fitter for the purpose, to accompany him by sea, whereby both all things would be no sooner put in readiness, and with less charge, and the emulation and division of command that might go between those kings of France and Spain, if they should both join the war by land upon Graecia, might be wisely avoided. And that for his part he would not be wanting in aids and contribution nothwithstanding if both these kings should refuse, rather than his Holiness should go alone he would wait upon him as soon as he could be ready. Always provided that he might first see all differences of the Christian princes amongst themselves fully laid down and appeased, as for his own part he was in none. And that he might have some good towns upon the coast in Italy put into his hands, for the retreat and safeguard of his men.'

With this answer Gasper Pons returned, nothing at all discontented.

And yet this declaration of the King (as superficial as it was) gave him that reputation abroad, as he was not long after elected by the Knights of the Rhodes protector of their order, all things multiplying to honour in a prince that had gotten such high estimation for his wisdom and sufficiency.

There were these two last years some proceedings against heretics, which was rare in this King's reign, and rather by penances than by fire. The King had (though he were no good schoolman) the honour to convert one of them by dispute at Canterbury.

This year also, though the King were no more haunted with sprites, for that by the sprinkling partly of blood and partly of water he had chased them away, yet nevertheless he had certain apparitions that troubled him, still showing themselves from one region, which was the house of York. It came so to pass that the Earl of Suffolk, son to Elizabeth, eldest sister to King Edward the Fourth by John Duke of Suffolk her second husband, and brother to John Earl of Lincoln, that was slain at Stokefield, being of a hasty and choleric disposition, had killed a man in his fury. Whereupon the King gave him his pardon, but either willing to leave a cloud upon him or the better to make him feel his grace, produced him openly to plead his pardon. This wrought in the Earl, as in a haughty stomach it uses to do. For the ignominy printed deeper than the grace. Wherefore, he being discontent, fled secretly into Flanders unto his aunt the Duchess of Burgundy. The King startled at it. But being taught by troubles to use fair and timely remedies, wrought so with him by messages (the Lady Margaret also growing by often failing in her alchemy weary of her experiments, and partly being a little sweetened for that the King had not touched her name in the confession of Perkin), that he came over again upon good terms, and was reconciled to the King.

In the beginning of the next year, being the seventeenth of the King, the Lady Catherine, fourth daughter of Ferdinando and Isabella, King and Queen of Spain, arrived in England at Plymouth the second of October, and was married to Prince Arthur in Paul's the fourteenth of November following, the Prince being then about fifteen years of age, and the lady about eighteen. The manner of her receiving, the manner of her entry into London, and the celebrity of the marriage were performed with great and true magnificence, in regard of cost, show, and order. The chief man that took the care was Bishop Fox, who was not only a grave counsellor for war or peace, but also a good surveyor of works and a good master of ceremonies, and anything else that was fit for the active part belonging to the service of court or state of a great King. This marriage was almost seven years in treaty, which was in part caused by the tender years of the marriage couple, especially of the Prince. But the true reason was that these two princes,[174] being princes of great policy and profound judgement, stood a great time looking upon another's fortunes, how they would go; knowing well that in the meantime the very treaty itself gave abroad in the world a reputation of a strait conjunction and amity between them, which served on both sides to many purposes that their several affairs required, and yet they continued still free. But in the end, when the fortunes of both the princes did grow every day more and more prosperous and assured, and that looking all about them they saw no better conditions, they shut it up.

The marriage-money the Princess brought (which was turned over to the King by act of renunciation) was 200,000 ducats, whereof 100,000 were payable ten days after the solemnisation and the other 100,000 at two payments annual, but part of it to be in jewels and plate, and a due course set down to have them justly and indifferently priced. The jointure or advancement of the lady was the third part of the principality of Wales, and of the dukedom of Cornwall, and of the earldom of Chester, to be after set forth in severalty. And in case she came to be queen of England her advancement was left indefinite, but thus, that it should be as great as ever any former queen of England had.

In all the devices and conceits of the triumphs of this marriage there was a great deal of astronomy, the lady being resembled to Hesperus, and the Prince to Arcturus,[175] and the old King Alphonsus[176] (that was the greatest astronomer of kings and was ancestor to the lady) was brought in to be the fortune-teller of the match. And whosoever had those toys in compiling, they were not altogether pedantical. But you may be sure that King Arthur the Briton, and the descent of the Lady Catherine from the house of Lancaster,[177] was in no wise forgotten. But as it should seem, it is not good to fetch fortunes from the stars. For this young prince (that drew upon him at that time not only the hopes and affections of his country but the eyes and expectation of foreigners) after a few months, in the beginning of April, deceased at Ludlow Castle, where he was sent to keep his resiance and court as Prince of Wales. Of this prince, in respect he died so young and by reason of his father's manner of education, which did cast no great lustre upon his children, there is little particular memory. Only thus much remains, that he was very studious and learned beyond his years and beyond the custom of great princes.

There was a doubt ripped up in the times following, when the divorce of King Henry the Eighth from the Lady Catherine did so much busy the world, whether Arthur was bedded with his lady or no, whereby that matter in fact (of carnal knowledge) might be made part of the case. And it is true that the lady herself denied it, or at least her counsel stood upon it, and would not blanch that advantage, although the plenitude of the Pope's power of dispensing[178] was the main question. And this doubt was kept long open in respect of the two queens that succeeded, Mary and Elizabeth,[179] whose legitimations were incompatible one with another, though their succession was settled by act of parliament. And the times that favoured Queen Mary's legitimation would have it believed that there was no carnal knowledge between Arthur and Catherine; not that they would seem to derogate from the Pope's absolute power to dispense even in that case, but only in point of honour and to make the case more favourable and smooth. And the times that favoured Queen Elizabeth's legitimation (which were the longer and the later) maintained the contrary. So much there remains in memory, that it was half a year's time between the creation of Henry Prince of Wales and Prince Arthur's death, which was construed to be, for to expect a full time whereby it might appear whether the Lady Catherine were with child by Prince Arthur or no. Again the lady herself procured a bull for the better corroboration of the marriage, with a clause of *vel forsan cognitam*,[180] which was not in the first bull. There was given in evidence also when the cause of the divorce was handled, pleasant passage, which was, that in a morning Prince Arthur upon his up-rising from bed with her called for drink, which he was not accustomed to do, and finding the gentleman of chamber that brought him the drink to smile at it and to note it, he said merrily to him that he had been in the midst of Spain, which was a hot region, and his journey had made him dry, and that if the other had been in so hot a clime he would have been drier than he. Besides the Prince was upon the point of sixteen years of age when he died, and forward, and able in body.

The February following, Henry Duke of York was created Prince of Wales, and Earl of Chester and Flint, for the Dukedom of Cornwall devolved to him by statute. The King, also being fast-handed and loath to part with a second dowry, but chiefly being affectionate both by his nature and out of politic considerations to continue the alliance with Spain, prevailed with the Prince (though not without some reluctation such as could be in those years, for he was not twelve years of age) to be contracted with the Princess Catherine, the secret providence of God ordaining that marriage to be the occasion of great events and changes.

The same year were the espousals of James King of Scotland with the Lady Margaret the King's eldest daughter, which was done by proxy and published at Paul's Cross the five and twentieth of January, and

Te Deum solemnly sung. But certain it is that the joy the city thereupon showed, by ringing of bells and bonfires and such other incense of the people, was more than could be expected in a case of so great and fresh enmity between the nations, especially in London, which was far enough off from feeling any of the former calamities of the war, and therefore might truly be attributed to a secret instinct and inspiring (which many times runs not only in the hearts of princes but in the pulse and veins of people) touching the happiness thereby to ensue in time to come. This marriage was in August following consummate at Edinburgh, the King bringing his daughter as far as Colliweston on the way, and then consigning her to the attendance of the Earl of Northumberland, who with a great troop of lords and ladies of honour brought her into Scotland to the King her husband.

This marriage had been in treaty by the space of almost three years, from the time that the King of Scotland did first open his mind to Bishop Fox. The sum given in marriage by the King was 10,000 pounds, and the jointure and advancement assured by the King of Scotland was 2,000 pounds a year after King James his death, and 1,000 pounds a year in present for the lady's allowance or maintenance, this to be set forth in lands, of the best and most certain revenue. During the treaty it is reported that the King remitted the matter to his council, and that some of the table in the freedom of counsellors (the King being present) did put the case that if God should take the King's two sons without issue, that then the kingdom of England would fall to the King of Scotland, which might prejudice the monarchy of England. Whereunto the King himself replied that if that should be, Scotland would be but an accession to England, and not England to Scotland, for that the greater would draw the less, and that it was a safer union for England than that of France. This passed as an oracle and silenced those that moved the question.

The same year was fatal as well for deaths as marriages, and that with equal temper. For the joys and feasts of the two marriages were compensed with the mournings and funerals of Prince Arthur (of whom we have spoken), and of Queen Elizabeth, who died in childbed in the Tower, and the child lived not long after. There died also that year Sir Reginald Bray, who was noted to have had with the King the greatest freedom of any counsellor, but it was but a freedom the better to set off flattery, yet he bore more than his just part of envy for the exactions.

At this time the King's estate was very prosperous: secured by the amity of Scotland; strengthened by that of Spain; cherished by that of Burgundy; all domestic troubles quenched; and all noise of war (like a thunder afar off) going upon Italy. Wherefore nature, which many times is happily contained and refrained by some bands of fortune, began to take place in the King, carrying as with a strong tide his affections and thoughts unto the gathering and heaping up of treasure. And as kings do more easily find instruments for their will and humour than for their service and honour, he had gotten for his purpose, or beyond his purpose two instruments, Empson and Dudley, whom the people esteemed as his horseleeches and shearers: bold men and careless of fame, and that took toll of the master's grist.

Dudley was of a good family, eloquent, and one that could put hateful business into good language. But Empson, that was the son of a sieve-maker, triumphed always upon the deed done, putting off all other respects whatsoever. These two persons, being lawyers in science and privy councillors in authority (as the corruption of the best things is the worst), turned law and justice into wormwood and rapine. For first their manner was to cause divers subjects to be indicted of sundry crimes, and so far forth to proceed in form of law, but when the bills were found,[181] then presently to commit them,[182] and nevertheless not to produce them in any reasonable time to their answer, but to suffer them to languish long in prison, and by sundry artificial devices and terrors to extort from them great fines and ransoms, which they termed compositions and mitigations.

Neither did they, towards the end, observe so much as the half-face[183] of justice in proceeding by indictment, but sent forth their precepts to attach men and convent[184] them before themselves and some others at their private houses, in a court of commission, and there used to shuffle up a summary proceeding by examination, without trial of jury, assuming to themselves there to deal both in pleas of the crown and controversies civil.

Then did they also use to enthral and charge the subjects' land with tenures *in capite*,[185] by finding false offices, and thereby to work upon them for wardships, liveries,[186] premier seisins[187] and alienations[188] (being the fruits of those tenures); refusing (upon divers pretexts and delays) to admit men to traverse those false offices, according to the law.

Nay, the King's wards after they had accomplished their full age could not be suffered to have livery of their lands without paying excessive fines, far exceeding all reasonable rates.

They did also vex men with information of intrusion, upon scarce colourable titles.[189]

When men were outlawed in personal actions[190] they would not permit them to purchase their charters of pardon except they paid great and intolerable sums, standing upon the strict point of law, which upon outlawries gives forfeiture of goods. Nay contrary to all law and colour, they maintained the King ought to have the half of men's lands and rents during the space of full two years, for a pain in case of outlawry. They would also ruffle with jurors and enforce them to find as they would direct, and (if they did not) convent them, imprison them, and fine them.

These and many other courses, fitter to be buried than repeated, they had of preying upon the people; both like tame hawks for their master, and like wild hawks for themselves, insomuch as they grew to great riches and substance. But their principal working was upon penal laws, wherein they spared none great nor small, nor considered whether the law were possible or impossible, in use or obsolete, but raked over all old and new statutes (though many of them were made with intention rather of terror than of rigour), ever having a rabble of promoters, questmongers, and leading jurors at their command, so as they could have anything found, either for fact or valuation.

There remains to this day a report that the King was on a time entertained by the Earl of Oxford (that was his principal servant both for war and peace) nobly and sumptuously, at his castle at Henningham. And at the King's going away, the Earl's servants stood in a seemly manner in their livery coats with cognisances, ranged on both sides, and made the King a lane. The King called the Earl to him and said, 'My lord, I have heard much of your hospitality, but I see it is greater than the speech. These handsome gentlemen and yeomen that I see on both sides of me are (sure) your menial servants.' The Earl smiled and said, 'It may please your grace, that were not for mine ease. They are most of them my retainers that are come to do me service at such a time as this and chiefly to see your grace.' The King started a little, and said, 'By my faith (my lord), I thank you for my good cheer, but I may not endure to have my laws broken in my sight.[191] My attorney must speak with you.' And it is part of the report, that the Earl compounded for no less than 15,000 marks.

And to show further the King's extreme diligence I do remember to have seen long since a book of account of Empson's, which had the King's hand almost to every leaf by way of signing, and was in some places postilled in the margin with the King's hand likewise, where was this remembrance:

> Item, Received, of such a one, five marks, for a pardon to be pro-cured; and if the pardon do not pass, the money to be repaid; except the party be some other ways satisfied.

And over against this memorandum (of the King's own hand):

> Otherwise satisfied.

Which I do the rather mention because it shows in the King a nearness, but yet with a kind of justness. So these little sands and grains of gold and silver (as it seems) helped not a little to make up the great heap and bank.

But meanwhile to keep the King awake, the Earl of Suffolk, having been too gay at Prince Arthur's marriage, and sunk himself deep in debt, had yet once more a mind to be a knight errant and to seek adventures in foreign parts, and taking his brother with him fled again into Flanders. That no doubt which gave him confidence was the great murmur of the people against the King's government. And being a man of a light and rash spirit, he thought every vapour would be a tempest. Neither wanted he some party within the kingdom. For the murmur of people awakes the discontents of nobles, and again that calls up commonly some head of sedition. The King resorting to his wonted and tried arts, caused Sir

Robert Curson, captain of the castle at Hammes (being at that time beyond sea, and therefore less likely to be wrought upon by the King), to fly from his charge and to feign himself a servant of the Earl's. This knight having insinuated himself into the secrets of the Earl, and finding by him upon whom chiefly he had either hope or hold, advertised the King thereof in great secrecy, but nevertheless maintained his own credit and inward trust with the Earl. Upon whose advertisements, the King attached William Courtney Earl of Devonshire, his brother-in-law, married to the Lady Katherine, daughter to King Edward the Fourth; William de la Pole, brother to the Earl of Suffolk; Sir James Tyrell and Sir John Windham, and some other meaner persons, and committed them to custody. George Lord Abergavenny and Sir Thomas Green were at the same time apprehended, but as upon less suspicion so in a freer restraint, and were soon after delivered. The Earl of Devonshire being interested[192] in the blood of York (that was rather feared than nocent), yet as one that might be the object of others' plots and designs, remained prisoner in the Tower during the King's life. William de la Pole was also long restrained, though not so straitly. But for Sir James Tyrell (against whom the blood of the innocent princes, Edward the Fifth and his brother, did still cry from under the altar[193]), and Sir John Windham, and the other meaner ones, they were attainted and executed, the two knights beheaded.

Nevertheless, to confirm the credit of Curson (who belike had not yet done all his feats of activity), there was published at Paul's Cross about the time of the said executions the Pope's bull of excommunication and curse against the Earl of Suffolk and Sir Robert Curson, and some others by name, and likewise in general against all the abettors of the said Earl, wherein it must be confessed that heaven was made too much to bow to earth, and religion to policy. But soon after, Curson when he saw time returned into England, and withal into wonted favour with the King, but worse fame with the people. Upon whose return the Earl was much dismayed, and seeing himself destitute of hopes (the Lady Margaret also by tract of time and bad success being now become cool in those attempts), after some wandering in France and Germany, and certain little projects (no better than squibs) of an exiled man, being tired out, retired again into the protection of the Archduke Philip in

Flanders, who by the death of Isabella was at that time King of Castile, in the right of Joan his wife.

This year, being the nineteenth of his reign, the King called his parliament, wherein a man may easily guess how absolute the King took himself to be with his parliament, when Dudley, that was so hateful, was made Speaker of the House of Commons. In this parliament there were not made many statutes memorable touching public government, but those that were had still the stamp of the King's wisdom and policy.

There was a statute made for the disannulling of all patents of lease or grant to such as came not upon lawful summons to serve the King in his wars against the enemies or rebels, or that should depart without the King's licence, with an exception of certain persons of the long-robe, providing nevertheless that they should have the King's wages from their house[194] till their return home again. There had been the like made before for offices, and by this statute it was extended to lands. But a man may easily see by many statutes made in this King's time that the King thought it safest to assist martial law by law of parliament.

Another statute was made prohibiting the bringing in of manufactures of silk wrought by itself or mixed with any other thread. But it was not of stuffs of whole piece (for that the realm had of them no manufacture in use at that time), but of knit silk or texture of silk, as ribbands, laces, cauls, points, and girdles, etc., which the people of England could then well skill to make. This law pointed at a true principle, that where foreign materials are but superfluities, foreign manufactures should be prohibited, for that will either banish the superfluity or gain the manufacture.

There was a law also of resumption of patents of gaols, and the reannexing of them to the sheriffwicks, privileged officers being no less an interruption of justice than privileged places.

There was likewise a law to restrain the by-laws or ordinances of corporations, which many times were against the prerogative of the King, the common law of the realm, and the liberty of the subject, being fraternities in evil. It was therefore provided that they should not be put in execution without the allowance of the Chancellor, treasurer, and the two chief justices, or three of them, or of the two justices of circuit where the corporation was.

Another law was in effect to bring in the silver of the realm to the mint, in making all clipped, minished or impaired coins of silver not to be current in payments, without giving any remedy of weight, but with an exception only of reasonable wearing (which was as nothing, in respect of the incertainty), and so upon the matter to set the mint on work, and to give way to new coins of silver that should be then minted.

There likewise was a long statute against vagabonds, wherein two things may be noted: the one, the dislike the parliament had of gaoling of them, as that which was chargeable, pesterous, and of no open example. The other, that in the statutes of this King's time (for this of the nineteenth year is not the only statute of that kind) there are ever coupled the punishment of vagabonds and the forbidding of dice and cards and unlawful games unto servants and mean people, and the putting down and suppressing of alehouses; as strings of one root together, and as if the one were unprofitable without the other.

As for riots and retainers, there passed scarce any parliament in this time without a law against them, the King ever having an eye to might and multitude.

There was granted also that parliament a subsidy, both from the temporalty and the clergy. And yet nevertheless ere the year expired there went out commissions for a general benevolence, though there were no wars, no fears. The same year the city gave 5,000 marks for confirmation of their liberties, a thing fitter for the beginnings of kings' reigns than the latter ends. Neither was it a small matter that the mint gained upon the late statute, by the recoinage of groats and half-groats, now twelvepences and sixpences.[195] As for Empson and Dudley's mills, they did grind more than ever. So that it was a strange thing to see what golden showers poured down upon the King's treasury at once: the last payments of the marriage money from Spain; the subsidy; the benevolence; the recoinage; the redemption of the city's liberties; the casualties.[196] And this is the more to be marvelled at because the King had then no occasions at all of wars or troubles. He had now but one son, and one daughter unbestowed. He was wise. He was of a high mind. He needed not to make riches his glory, he did excel in so many things else, save that certainly avarice does ever find in itself matter of ambition. Belike he thought to leave his son such a kingdom and such a mass of treasure, as he might choose his greatness where he would.

This year was also kept the Serjeants' feast, which was the second call in this King's days.

About this time Isabella Queen of Castile deceased, a right noble lady and an honour to her sex and times, and the cornerstone of the greatness of Spain that has followed. This accident the King took not for news at large, but thought it had a great relation to his own affairs, especially in two points: the one for example, the other for consequence. First, he conceived that the case of Ferdinando of Aragon after the death of Queen Isabella was his own case after the death of his own queen; and the case of Joan the heir unto Castile was the case of his own son Prince Henry. For if both of the kings had their kingdoms in the right of their wives, they descended to the heirs and did not accrue to the husbands. And although his own case had both steel and parchment more than the other, that is to say, a conquest in the field and an act of parliament, yet notwithstanding, that natural title of descent in blood did (in the imagination even of a wise man) breed a doubt that the other two were not safe nor sufficient. Wherefore he was wonderful diligent to enquire and observe what became of the King of Aragon in holding and continuing the kingdom of Castile, and whether he did hold it in his own right or as administrator to his daughter, and whether he were like to hold it in fact or to be put out by his son-in-law.

Secondly, he did revolve in his mind that the state of Christendom might by this late accident have a turn. For whereas before time himself with the conjunction of Aragon and Castile (which then was one), and the amity of Maximilian and Philip his son the Archduke, was far too strong a party for France, he began to fear that now the French King (who had great interest in the affection of Philip, the young King of Castile), and Philip himself now King of Castile (who was in ill terms with his father-in-law about the present government of Castile), and thirdly Maximilian, Philip's father (who was ever variable, and upon whom the surest aim that could be taken was that he would not be long as he had been last before), would all three, being potent princes, enter into some strait league and confederation amongst themselves, whereby though he should not be endangered yet he should be left to the poor amity of Aragon; and whereas he had been heretofore a kind of arbiter of Europe, he should now go less, and be over-topped by so great a conjunction.

He had also (as it seems) an inclination to marry, and bethought himself of some fit conditions abroad. And amongst others he had heard of the beauty and virtuous behaviour of the young Queen of Naples, the widow of Ferdinando the younger, being then of matronal years of seven and twenty, by whose marriage he thought that the kingdom of Naples, having been a goal for a time between the King of Aragon and the French King, and being but newly settled might in some part be deposited in his hands, who was so able to keep the stakes. Therefore he sent in ambassage or message three confident persons, Francis Marsin, James Braybrooke, and John Stile, upon two several inquisitions, rather than negotiations, the one touching the person and condition of the young Queen of Naples, the other touching all particulars of estate that concerned the fortunes and intentions of Ferdinando. And because they may observe best who themselves are observed least, he sent them under colourable pretexts, giving them letters of kindness and compliment from Catherine the Princess to her aunt and niece, the old and young Queen of Naples, and delivering to them also a book of new articles of peace, which, notwithstanding it had been delivered unto Doctor de Puebla, the lieger ambassador of Spain here in England, to be sent, yet for that the King had been long without hearing from Spain he thought good those messengers, when they had been with the two queens, should likewise pass on to the court of Ferdinando and take a copy of the book with them .

The instructions touching the Queen of Naples were so curious and exquisite, being as articles whereby to direct a survey or framing a particular of her person, for complexion, favour, feature, stature, health, age, customs, behaviour, conditions, and estate; as, if the King had been young, a man would have judged him to be amorous, but being ancient it ought to be interpreted that sure he was very chaste, for that he meant to find all things in one woman and so to settle his affections without ranging. But in this match he was soon cooled when he heard from his ambassadors that this young queen had had a goodly jointure in the realm of Naples, well answered during the time of her uncle Frederick, yea and during the time of Lewis the French King, in whose division her revenue fell; but since the time that the kingdom was in Ferdinando's hands all was assigned to the army and garrisons there, and she received only a pension or exhibition out of his coffers.

The other part of the enquiry had a grave and diligent return, informing the King at full of the present state of King Ferdinando. By this report it appeared to the King that Ferdinando did continue the government of Castile as administrator unto his daughter Joan, by the title of Queen Isabella's will, and partly by the custom of the kingdom (as he pretended), and that all mandates and grants were expedited in the name of Joan his daughter and himself as administrator, without mention of Philip her husband. And that King Ferdinando, howsoever he did dismiss himself of the name of King of Castile, yet meant to hold the kingdom without account and in absolute command.

It appears also that he flattered himself with hopes that King Philip would permit unto him the government of Castile during his life, which he had laid his plot to work him unto, both by some counsellors of his about him that Ferdinando had at his devotion, and chiefly by promise that in case Philip gave not way unto it he would marry some young lady, whereby to put him by[197] the succession of Aragon and Granada, in case he[198] should have a son; and lastly by representing unto him that the government of the Burgundians, till Philip were by continuance in Spain made as natural of Spain, would not be endured by the Spaniards. But in all those things, though wisely laid down and considered, Ferdinando failed; but that Pluto was better to him than Pallas.[199]

In the same report also the ambassadors, being mean men[200] and therefore the more free, did strike upon a string that was somewhat dangerous, for they declared plainly that the people of Spain, both nobles and commons, were better affected unto the part of Philip (so he brought his wife with him) than to Ferdinando, and expressed the reason to be because he[201] had imposed upon them many taxes and tallages, which was the King's own case between him and his son.[202]

There was also in this report a declaration of an overture of marriage that Amason the secretary of Ferdinando had made unto the ambassadors in great secret, between Charles Prince of Castile and Mary the King's second daughter; assuring the King that the treaty of marriage then on foot for the said prince and the daughter of France would break, and that she the said daughter of France should be married to Angoulême, that was the heir apparent of France.

There was a touch also of a speech of marriage between Ferdinando and Madame de Foix, a lady of the blood of France, which afterwards indeed succeeded. But this was reported as learnt in France, and silenced in Spain.

The King by the return of this ambassage, which gave great light unto his affairs, was well instructed and prepared how to carry himself between Ferdinando King of Aragon and Philip his son-in-law, King of Castile, resolving with himself to do all that in him lay to keep them at one within themselves, but howsoever that succeeded, by a moderate carriage and bearing the person of a common friend to lose neither of their friendships; but yet to run a course more entire with the King of Aragon, but more laboured and officious with the King of Castile. But he was much taken with the overture of marriage with his daughter Mary, both because it was the greatest marriage of Christendom and for that it took hold of both allies.

But to corroborate his alliance with Philip, the winds gave him an interview. For Philip, choosing the winter season the better to surprise the King of Aragon, set forth with a great navy out of Flanders for Spain in the month of January, the one and twentieth year of the King's reign. But himself was surprised with a cruel tempest, that scattered his ships upon the several coasts of England, and the ship wherein the King and Queen were, with two other small barks only, torn and in great peril, to escape the fury of the weather thrust into Weymouth. King Philip himself, having not been used as it seems to sea, all wearied and extreme sick, would needs land to refresh his spirits, though it was against the opinion of his council, doubting it might breed delay, his occasions requiring celerity.

The rumour of the arrival of a puissant navy upon the coast made the country arm. And Sir Thomas Trenchard, with forces suddenly raised, not knowing what the matter might be came to Weymouth, where, understanding the accident, he did in all humbleness and humanity invite the King and Queen to his house, and forthwith despatched posts to the court. Soon after came Sir John Caroe likewise with a great troop of men well armed, using the like humbleness and respects towards the King when he knew the case. King Philip doubting that they, being but subjects, dared not let him pass away again without the King's notice and leave, yielded to their entreaties to stay till they heard from the court. The King, as soon as he heard the news commanded presently the Earl of Arundel to go to visit the King of Castile, and to let him understand that as he was very sorry for his mishap, so he was glad that he had escaped the danger of the seas, and likewise of the occasion himself had to do him honour; and desiring him to think himself as in his own land, and that the King made all haste possible to come and embrace him.

The Earl came to him in great magnificence with a brave troop of 300 horse; and for more state came by torchlight. After he had done the King's message, King Philip seeing how the world went, the sooner to get away went upon speed to the King at Windsor, and his queen followed by easy journeys. The two kings at their meeting used all the caresses and loving demonstrations that were possible. And the King of Castile said pleasantly to the King that he was now punished for that he would not come within his walled town of Calais, when they met last. But the King answered that walls and seas were nothing where hearts were open, and that he[203] was here no otherwise but to be served.

After a day or two's refreshing the kings entered into speech of renewing the treaty, the King saying that though King Philip's person were the same, yet his fortunes and state were raised, in which case a renovation of treaty was used amongst princes. But while these things were in handling the King, choosing a fit time, and drawing the King of Castile into a room where they two only were private, and laying his hand civilly upon his arm, and changing his countenance a little from a countenance of entertainment, said to him, 'Sir, you have been saved upon my coast, I hope you will not suffer me to wreck upon yours.' The King of Castile asked him what he meant by that speech? 'I mean it' (says the King) 'by that same harebrain wild fellow my subject the Earl of Suffolk, who is protected in your country, and begins to play the fool when all others are weary of it.' The King of Castile answered, 'I had thought, Sir, your felicity had been above those thoughts. But if it trouble you I will banish him.' The King replied, those hornets were best in their nest, and worst then when they did fly abroad; and that his desire was to have him delivered to him. The King of Castile herewith a little confused, and in a study,[204] said, 'That can I not do with my honour, and less with yours; for you will be thought to have used me as a prisoner.' The King presently said, 'Then the matter is at an end. For I will take that dishonour upon me, and so your honour is saved.'

The King of Castile (who had the King in great estimation, and besides remembered where he was, and knew not what use he might have of the King's amity, for that himself was new in his state of Spain, and unsettled both with his father-in-law and with his people) composing his countenance said, 'Sir, you give law to me; but so will I to you. You shall have him, but upon your honour you shall not take his life.' The King embracing him said, 'Agreed.' Says the King of Castile, 'Neither shall it dislike you if I send to him in such a fashion as he may partly come with his own good will.' The King said it was well thought of, and if it pleased him he would join with him in sending to the Earl a message to that purpose. They both sent severally, and meanwhile they continued feasting and pastimes, the King being on his part willing to have the Earl sure before the King of Castile went, and the King of Castile being as willing to seem to be enforced. The King also with many wise and excellent persuasions did advise the King of Castile to be ruled by the counsel of his father-in-law Ferdinando, a prince so prudent, so experienced, so fortunate. The King of Castile (who was in no very good terms with his said father-in-law) answered, that if his father-in-law would suffer him to govern his kingdoms, he should govern him.[205]

There were immediately messengers sent from both kings to recall the Earl of Suffolk, who upon gentle words used to him was soon charmed, and willing enough to return, assured of his life and hoping of his liberty. He was brought through Flanders to Calais, and thence landed at Dover, and with sufficient guard delivered and received at the Tower of London. Meanwhile King Henry to draw out the time, continued his feastings and entertainments, and after he had received the King of Castile into the fraternity of the Garter, and for a reciprocal had his son the Prince admitted to the order of the Golden Fleece, he accompanied King Philip and his queen to the city of London, where they were entertained with the greatest magnificence and triumph that could be upon no greater warning. And as soon as the Earl of Suffolk had been conveyed to the Tower (which was the serious part) the jollities had an end, and the kings took leave. Nevertheless during their being here they in substance concluded that treaty which the Flemings term *intercursus malus*, and bears date at Windsor, for that there be some things in it more to the advantage of the English than of them, especially for that the free fishing of the Dutch upon the coasts and seas of England, granted in the treaty of *undecimo*,[206] was not by this treaty confirmed, all articles that confirm former treaties being precisely and warily limited and confined to matter of commerce only, and not otherwise.

It was observed that the great tempest that drove Philip into England blew down the golden eagle from the spire of Paul's, and in the fall it fell upon a sign of the black eagle that was in Paul's churchyard, in the place where the schoolhouse now stands, and battered it and broke it down, which was a strange stooping of a hawk upon a fowl. This the people interpreted to be an ominous prognostic upon the imperial house, which was by interpretation also fulfilled upon Philip the Emperor's son, not only in the present disaster of the tempest but in that that followed. For Philip arriving into Spain and attaining the possession of the kingdom of Castile without resistance (insomuch as Ferdinando, who had spoke so great before, was with difficulty admitted to the speech of his son-in-law), sickened soon after, and deceased, yet after such time as there was an observation by the wisest of that court that if he had lived his father would have gained upon him in that sort as he would have governed his counsels and designs, if not his affections. By this all Spain returned into the power of Ferdinando in state as it was before, the rather in regard of the infirmity of Joan his daughter, who loving her husband (by whom she had many children) dearly well, and no less beloved of him (howsoever her father, to make Philip ill-beloved of the people of Spain, gave out that Philip used her not well), was unable in strength of mind to bear the grief of his decease and fell distracted of her wits; of which malady her father was thought no ways to endeavour the cure, the better to hold his regal power in Castile. So that as the felicity of Charles the Eighth was said to be a dream, so the adversity of Ferdinando was said likewise to be a dream, it passed over so soon.

About this time the King was desirous to bring into the house of Lancaster celestial honour, and became suitor to Pope Julius to canonise King Henry the Sixth for a saint, the rather in respect of that his famous prediction of the King's own assumption to the crown. Julius referred the matter (as the manner is) to certain cardinals to take the verification of his holy acts and miracles, but it died under the reference. The general opinion was that Pope Julius was too dear, and that the King would not come to his rates. But it is more probable that that Pope, who was extremely jealous of the dignity of the see of Rome and of the acts thereof, knowing that King Henry the Sixth was reputed in the world abroad but for a simple man, was afraid it would but diminish the estimation of that kind of honour if there were not a distance kept between innocents and saints.

The same year likewise there proceeded a treaty of marriage between the King and the Lady Margaret, Duchess Dowager of Savoy, only daughter to Maximilian and sister to the King of Castile, a lady wise and of great good fame. This matter had been in speech between the two kings at their meeting, but was soon after resumed, and therein was employed for his first piece the King's then chaplain, and after the great prelate, Thomas Wolsey.[207] It was in the end concluded with great and ample conditions for the King, but with promise *de futuro*[208] only. It may be the King was the rather induced unto it for that he had heard more and more of the marriage to go on between his great friend and ally Ferdinando of Aragon and Madame de Foix, whereby that King began to piece with the French King, from whom he had been always before severed. So fatal a thing it is for the greatest and straitest amities of kings at one time or other to have a little of the wheel.[209] Nay there is a further tradition (in Spain though not with us) that the King of Aragon (after he knew that the marriage between Charles the young Prince of Castile and Mary the King's second daughter went roundly on, which though it was first moved by the King of Aragon, yet it was afterwards wholly advanced and brought to perfection by Maximilian and the friends on that side), entered into a jealousy that the King did aspire to the government of Castilia, as administrator during the minority of his son-in-law, as if there should have been a competition of three for that government: Ferdinando grandfather on the mother's side, Maximilian grandfather on the father's side, and King Henry father-in-law to the young prince.

Certainly it is not unlike but the King's government (carrying the young prince with him) would have been perhaps more welcome to the Spaniards than that of the other two. For the nobility of Castilia, that so lately put out the King of Aragon in favour of King Philip, and had discovered themselves so far, could not be but in a secret distrust and distaste of that King. And as for Maximilian, upon twenty respects he could not have been the man. But this purpose of the King's seems to me (considering the King's safe courses, never found to be enterprising or adventurous) not greatly probable, except he should have had a desire to breathe warmer, because he had ill lungs.

This marriage with Margaret was protracted from time to time in respect of the infirmity of the King, who now in the two and twentieth of his reign began to be troubled with the gout. But the defluxion taking also into his breast wasted his lungs, so that thrice in a year in a kind of return, and especially in the spring, he had great fits and labours of the tissick. Nevertheless he continued to intend business with as great diligence as before in his health, yet so, as upon this warning he did likewise now more seriously think of the world to come, and of making himself a saint, as well as King Henry the Sixth, by treasure better employed than to be given to Pope Julius. For this year he gave greater alms than accustomed, and discharged all prisoners about the city that lay for fees, or debts under forty shillings. He did also make haste with religious foundations and in the year following, which was the three and twentieth, finished that of the Savoy.[210] And hearing also of the bitter cries of his people against the oppressions of Dudley and Empson and their complices, partly by devout persons about him and partly by public sermons (the preachers doing their duty therein), he was touched with great remorse for the same.

Nevertheless Empson and Dudley, though they could not but hear of these scruples in the King's conscience, yet as if the King's soul and his money were in several offices, that the one was not to intermeddle with the other, went on with as great rage as ever. For the same three and twentieth year was there a sharp prosecution against Sir William Capel (now the second time), and this was for matters of misgovernment in his mayoralty; the great matter being that in some payments he had taken knowledge of false moneys, and did not his diligence to examine and beat it out who were the offenders. For this and some other things laid to his charge he was condemned to pay 2,000 pounds, and being a man of stomach and hardened by his former troubles, refused to pay a mite; and belike used some untoward speeches of the proceedings, for which he was sent to the Tower, and there remained till the King's death. Knesworth likewise, that had been lately Mayor of London, and both his Sheriffs, were for abuses in their offices questioned and imprisoned, and delivered upon 1,400 pounds paid. Hawis, an Alderman of London, was put in trouble, and died with thought and anguish before his business came to an end. Sir Laurence Ailmer, who had likewise been Mayor of London, and his two Sheriffs, were put to the fine of 1,000 pounds. And Sir Laurence for refusing to make payment was committed to prison, where he stayed till Empson himself was committed in his place.

It is no marvel (if the faults were so light and the rates so heavy) that the King's treasure of store that he left at his death, most of it in secret places under his own key and keeping at Richmond, amounted (as by tradition it is reported to have done) unto the sum of near eighteen hundred thousand pounds sterling; a huge mass of money even for these times.

The last act of state that concluded this King's temporal felicity was the conclusion of a glorious match between his daughter Mary and Charles Prince of Castile, afterwards the great Emperor, both being of tender years, which treaty was perfected by Bishop Fox and other his commissioners at Calais, the year before the King's death. In which alliance it seems he himself took so high contentment, as in a letter that he wrote thereupon to the city of London commanding all possible demonstrations of joy to be made for the same, he expresses himself as if he thought he had built a wall of brass about his kingdom, when he had for his sons-in-law a king of Scotland and a prince of Castile and Burgundy. So as now there was nothing to be added to this great King's felicity, being at the top of all worldly bliss, in regard of the high marriages of his children, his great renown throughout Europe, and his scarce credible riches, and the perpetual constancy of his prosperous successes, but an opportune death, to withdraw him from any future blow of fortune, which certainly (in regard of the great hatred of his people and the title of his son, being then come to eighteen years of age, and being a bold prince and liberal, and that gained upon the people by his very aspect and presence) had not been impossible to have come upon him.

To crown also the last year of his reign as well as his first, he did an act of piety, rare and worthy to be taken in imitation. For he granted forth a general pardon, as expecting a second coronation in a better kingdom. He did also declare in his will, that his mind was, that restitution should be made of those sums that had been unjustly taken by his officers.

And thus this Solomon of England (for Solomon also was too heavy upon his people in exactions) having lived two and fifty years, and thereof reigned three and twenty years and eight months, being in perfect memory and in a most blessed mind, in a great calm of a consuming sickness, passed to a better world, the two and twentieth of April 1508, at his palace of Richmond, which himself had built.

This king (to speak of him in terms equal to his deserving) was one of the best sort of wonders, a wonder for wise men. He had parts (both in his virtues and his fortune) not so fit for a commonplace as for observation. Certainly he was religious, both in his affection and observance. But as he could see clear (for those times) through superstition, so he would be blinded now and then by human policy. He advanced churchmen; he was tender in the privilege of sanctuaries, though they wrought him much mischief; he built and endowed many religious foundations, besides his memorable hospital of the Savoy; and yet was he a great almsgiver in secret, which showed that his works in public were dedicated rather to God's glory than his own. He professed always to love and seek peace, and it was his usual preface in his treaties that when Christ came into the world peace was sung, and when he went out of the world peace was bequeathed. And this virtue could not proceed out of fear or softness, for he was valiant and active, and therefore no doubt it was truly Christian and moral. Yet he knew the way to peace was not to seem to be desirous to avoid wars. Therefore would he make offers and fames of wars, till he had mended the conditions of peace.

It was also much, that one that was so great a lover of peace should be so happy in war. For his arms, either in foreign or civil wars, were never unfortunate, neither did he know what a disaster meant. The war of his coming in, and the rebellions of the Earl of Lincoln and the Lord Audley, were ended by victory; the wars of France and Scotland, by peaces sought at his hands; that of Brittany, by accident of the Duke's death; the insurrection of the Lord Lovel, and that of Perkin at Exeter and in Kent, by flight of the rebels before they came to blows; so that his fortune of arms was still inviolate. The rather sure, for that in the quenching of the commotions of his subjects he ever went in person, sometimes reserving himself to back and second his lieutenants, but ever in action. And yet that was not merely forwardness, but partly distrust of others.

He did much maintain and countenance his laws, which (nevertheless) was no impediment to him to work his will. For it was so handled that neither prerogative nor profit went to diminution. And yet as he would sometimes strain up his laws to his prerogative, so would he also let down his prerogative to his parliament, for mint and wars and martial discipline (things of absolute power) he would nevertheless bring to parliament. Justice was well administered in his time, save where the King was party; save also that the council-table intermeddled too much with *meum* and *tuum*.[211] For it was a very court of justice during his time, especially in the beginning. But in that part both of justice and policy, which is the making of good laws, he did excel.

And with his justice he was also a merciful prince, as in whose time there were but three of the nobility that suffered: the Earl of Warwick, the Lord Chamberlain, and the Lord Audley; though the first two were instead of numbers in the dislike and obloquy of the people. But there were never so great rebellions expiated with so little blood drawn by the hand of justice as the two rebellions of Blackheath and Exeter. As for the severity used upon those that were taken in Kent, it was but upon a scum of people. His pardons went ever both before and after his sword. But then he had withal a strange kind of interchanging of large and unexpected pardons with severe executions, which (his wisdom considered) could not be imputed to any inconstancy or inequality, but either to some reason that we do not now know, or to a principle he had set unto himself, that he would vary and try both ways in turn.

But the less blood he drew the more he took of treasure, and as some construed it, he was the more sparing in the one that he might be the more pressing in the other, for both would have been intolerable. Of nature assuredly he coveted to accumulate treasure, and was a little poor in admiring riches. The people (into whom there is infused for the preservation of monarchies a natural desire to discharge their princes,[212] though it be with the unjust charge of their counsellors and ministers) did impute this unto Cardinal Morton and Sir Reginald Bray; who as it after appeared (as counsellors of ancient authority with him) did so second his humours, as nevertheless they did temper them. Whereas Empson and Dudley that followed, being persons that had no reputation with him otherwise than by the servile following of his bent, did not give way only (as the first did) but shape him way to those extremities, for which himself was touched with remorse at his death, and which his successor renounced, and sought to purge.

This excess of his had at that time many glosses and interpretations. Some thought the continual rebellions wherewith he had been vexed had made him grow to hate his people; some thought it was done to pull down their stomachs and to keep them low; some, for that he would leave his son a golden fleece; some suspected he had some high design upon foreign parts. But those perhaps shall come nearest the truth that fetch not their reasons so far off, but rather impute it to nature, age, peace, and a mind fixed upon no other ambition or pursuit. Whereunto I should add that, having every day occasion to take notice of the necessities and shifts for money of other great princes abroad, it did the better by comparison set off to him the felicity of full coffers. As to his expending of treasure he never spared charge that his affairs required, and in his buildings was magnificent, but his rewards were very limited. So that his liberality was rather upon his own state and memory than upon the deserts of others.

He was of a high mind, and loved his own will and his own way, as one that revered himself, and would reign indeed. Had he been a private man he would have been termed proud, but in a wise prince, it was but keeping of distance, which indeed he did towards all, not admitting any near or full approach either to his power or to his secrets, for he was governed by none. His queen (notwithstanding she had presented him with divers children, and with a crown also, though he would not acknowledge it) could do nothing with him. His mother he reverenced much, heard little. For any person agreeable to him for society (such as was Hastings to King Edward the Fourth, or Charles Brandon after to King Henry the Eighth), he had none, except we should account for such persons Fox and Bray and Empson, because they were so much with him. But it was but as the instrument is much with the workman. He had nothing in him of vainglory, but yet kept state and majesty to the height, being sensible that majesty makes the people bow, but vainglory bows to them.

To his confederates abroad he was constant and just, but not open. But rather such was his inquiry and such his closeness as they stood in the light towards him, and he stood in the dark to them; yet without strangeness, but with a semblance of mutual communication of affairs. As for little envies or emulations upon foreign princes (which are frequent with many kings), he had never any, but went substantially to his own business, Certain it is, that though his reputation was great at home yet it was greater abroad. For foreigners that could not see the passages of affairs, but made their judgements upon the issues of them, noted that he was ever in strife and ever aloft. It grew also from the airs that the princes and states abroad received from their ambassadors and agents here, which were attending the court in great number, whom he did not only content with courtesy, reward, and privateness, but (upon such conferences as passed with them) put them in admiration to find his universal insight into the affairs of the world, which, though he did suck chiefly from themselves, yet that which he had gathered from them all seemed admirable to everyone. So that they did write ever to their superiors in high terms concerning his wisdom and art of rule. Nay when they were returned, they did commonly maintain intelligence with him, such a dexterity he had to impropriate to himself all foreign instruments.

He was careful and liberal to obtain good intelligence from all parts abroad, wherein he did not only use his interest in the liegers here, and his pensioners[213] that he had both in the court of Rome and other the courts of Christendom, but the industry and vigilancy of his own ambassadors in foreign parts. For which purpose his instructions were ever extreme curious and articulate, and in them more articles touching inquisition than touching negotiation, requiring likewise from his ambassadors an answer in particular distinct articles, respectively to his questions.

As for his secret spials that he did employ both at home and abroad, by them to discover what practices and conspiracies were against him, surely his case required it, he had such moles perpetually working and casting to undermine him. Neither can it be reprehended, for if spials be lawful against lawful enemies, much more against conspirators and traitors. But indeed to give them credence by oaths or curses,[214] that cannot be well maintained, for those are too holy vestments for a disguise. Yet surely there was this further good in his employing of these flies and familiars, that as the use of them was cause that many conspiracies were revealed, so the fame and suspicion of them kept (no doubt) many conspiracies from being attempted.

Towards his queen he was nothing uxorious, nor scarce indulgent, but companiable and respective, and without jealousy. Towards his children he was full of paternal affection, careful of their education, aspiring to their high advancement, regular to see that they should not want of any due honour and respect, but not greatly willing to cast any popular lustre upon them.

To his council he did refer much, and sat oft in person, knowing it to be the way to assist his power and inform his judgement, in which respect also he was fairly patient of liberty both of advice and of vote, till himself were declared.

He kept a strait hand on his nobility, and chose rather to advance clergymen and lawyers, which were more obsequious to him but had less interest in the people, which made for his absoluteness, but not for his safety. Insomuch as I am persuaded it was one of the causes of his troublesome reign, for that his nobles, though they were loyal and obedient, yet did not co-operate with him but let every man go his own way. He was not afraid of an able man, as Lewis the Eleventh was. But contrariwise, he was served by the ablest men that then were to be found, without which his affairs could not have prospered as they did. For war, Bedford, Oxford, Surrey, Daubeney, Brooke, Poynings. For other affairs, Morton, Fox, Bray, the Prior of Llanthony, Warham, Urswick, Hussey, Frowick, and others. Neither did he care how cunning they were that he did employ, for he thought himself to have the master-reach. And as he chose well, so he held them up well. For it is a strange thing, that though he were a dark prince, and infinitely suspicious, and his times full of secret conspiracies and troubles, yet in twenty-four years' reign he never put down or discomposed counsellor or near servant, save only Stanley the Lord Chamberlain. As for the disposition of his subjects in general towards him, it stood thus with him, that of the three affections that naturally tie the hearts of the subjects to their sovereign – love, fear, and reverence – he had the last in height; the second in good measure; and so little of the first as he was beholding to the other two.

He was a prince, sad, serious, and full of thoughts and secret observations; and full of notes and memorials of his own hand, specially touching persons, as whom to employ, whom to reward, whom to enquire of, whom to beware of, what were the dependencies, what were the factions, and the like; keeping (as it were) a journal of his thoughts. There is to this day a merry tale that his monkey (set on as it was thought by one of his chamber) tore his principal notebook all to pieces, when by chance it lay forth, whereat the court that liked not those pensive accounts was almost tickled with sport.

He was indeed full of apprehensions and suspicions. But as he did easily take them, so he did easily check them and master them, whereby they were not dangerous, but troubled himself more than others. It is true, his thoughts were so many as they could not well always stand together; but that which did good one way, did hurt another. Neither did he at some times weigh them aright in their proportions. Certainly that rumour that did him so much mischief (that the Duke of York should be saved and alive) was (at the first) of his own nourishing, because he would have more reason not to reign in the right of his wife. He was affable, and both well and fair spoken, and would use strange sweetness and blandishments of words where he desired to effect or persuade any thing that he took to heart. He was rather studious than learned, reading most books that were of any worth in the French tongue. Yet he understood the Latin, as appears in that Cardinal Hadrian and others, who could very well have written French, did use to write to him in Latin.

For his pleasures, there is no news of them. And yet by his instructions to Marsin and Stile touching the Queen of Naples, it seems he could interrogate well touching beauty. He did by pleasures as great princes do by banquets, come and look a little upon them, and turn way. For never prince was more wholly given to his affairs, nor in them more of himself; insomuch as in triumphs of jousts and tourneys and balls and masks (which they then called disguises) he was rather a princely and gentle spectator than seemed much to be delighted.

No doubt, in him as in all men (and most of all in kings) his fortune wrought upon his nature, and his nature upon his fortune. He attained to the crown not only from a private fortune, which might endow him with moderation, but also from the fortune of an exiled man, which had quickened in him all seeds of observation and industry. And his times being rather prosperous than calm, had raised his confidence by success but almost marred his nature by troubles. His wisdom, by often evading from perils, was turned rather into a dexterity to deliver himself from dangers when they pressed him than into a providence to prevent and remove them afar off. And even in nature, the sight of his mind was like some sights of eyes, rather strong at hand than to carry afar off. For his wit increased upon the occasion, and so much the more if the occasion were sharpened by danger.

Again, whether it were the shortness of his foresight, or the strength of his will, or the dazzling of his suspicions, or what it was, certain it is that the perpetual troubles of his fortunes (there being no more matter out of which they grew) could not have been without some great defects and main errors in his nature, customs and proceedings, which he had enough to do to save and help with a thousand little industries and watches. But those do best appear in the story itself. Yet take him with all his defects, if a man should compare him with the kings his concurrents in France and Spain, he shall find him more politic than

Lewis the Twelfth of France, and more entire and sincere than Ferdinando of Spain. But if you shall change Lewis the Twelfth for Lewis the Eleventh, who lived a little before, then the consort is more perfect. For that Lewis the Eleventh, Ferdinando, and Henry, may be esteemed for the *tres magi*[215] of kings of those ages. To conclude, if this King did no greater matters, it was long of himself, for what he minded he compassed.

He was a comely personage, a little above just stature, well and straight limbed, but slender. His countenance was reverend, and a little like a churchman; and as it was not strange or dark so neither was it winning or pleasing, but as the face of one well disposed. But it was to the disadvantage of the painter, for it was best when he spoke.

His worth may bear a tale or two, that may put upon him somewhat that may seem divine. When the Lady Margaret his mother had divers great suitors for marriage, she dreamed one night that one in the likeness of a bishop in pontifical habit did tender her Edmund, Earl of Richmond (the King's father) for her husband. Neither had she ever any child but the King, though she had three husbands.

One day when King Henry the Sixth (whose innocency gave him holiness) was washing his hands at a great feast, and cast his eye upon King Henry, then a young youth, he said, 'This is the lad that shall possess quietly that that we now strive for.' But that that was truly divine in him, was that he had the fortune of a true Christian as well as of a great king, in living exercised and dying repentant. So as he had a happy warfare in both conflicts, both of sin and the cross.

He was born at Pembroke Castle, and lies buried at Westminster, in one of the stateliest and daintiest monuments of Europe, both for the chapel and for the sepulchre. So that he dwells more richly dead in the moment of his tomb, than he did alive in Richmond or any of his palaces. I could wish he did the like in this monument of his fame.

NOTES

1. Richard Duke of Gloucester (1452–85), the youngest son of Richard, Duke of York, and the last king of the House of York. After the death of his brother, Edward IV, Richard governed as regent for Edward's son Edward V, before putting Edward and his brother in the Tower and making himself king. He was killed fighting Henry Tudor (later Henry VII) at the battle of Bosworth in 1485. His defeat ended the Wars of the Roses.

2. Henry Tudor (1457–1509), grandson of Owen Tudor and Catherine of Valois, the widow of Henry V. King of England 1485–1509.

3. Henry VI (1421–71), King of England 1422–61, the only child of Henry V and Catherine of Valois. His nominal rule ended when Edward IV returned to London in 1471, and after the Yorkist victory at Tewkesbury in 1471, where his only son was killed, he was murdered in the Tower.

4. George, Duke of Clarence (1449–78), the third son of Richard, Duke of York, and brother of Edward IV and Richard III. In 1478 he was accused of treason by his brothers, and executed.

5. Edward IV's sons, Edward V and his younger brother, Richard, 'the Princes in the Tower'. They were placed in the Tower by Richard III, and never heard of again, presumably murdered on their uncle's orders, though other theories abound.

6. It was rumoured that Richard wanted to marry Elizabeth of York (his niece, and thus 'within the degrees forbidden'), who was already betrothed to the future King Henry VII.

7. Treaty made at Picquigny in 1475.

8. Edward IV's wife Elizabeth Woodville, whom he had married secretly in 1464, was not of noble blood.

9. i.e. a right to the throne.

10. Elizabeth of York (1465–1503), eldest daughter of Edward IV (see note 6).

11. i.e. through both descent and occupation of the throne.

12. Edward IV (1442–83), eldest son of Richard Duke of York, King of England 1461–83.

13. i.e. an act of parliament.

14. Edward V and Richard, Duke of York (see note 5).

15. In 1461 parliament rejected the right of the house of Lancaster to the throne. Henry VI was allowed to reign during his lifetime, to be succeeded by the house of York.

16. William I, known as the Conqueror (c.1028–87), Duke of Normandy and the first Norman king of England (1066–87).

17. St Edward the Confessor (c.1003–66), King of England 1042–66.

18. Kings Henry IV, Henry V and Henry VI.

19. Edward Plantagenet, Earl of Warwick and Earl of Salisbury (1475–99), potential claimant to the English throne during the reigns of both Richard III and Henry VII.

20. In 1483 Richard hired Dr Shaw to preach against the legitimacy of the children of Edward IV, thereby asserting his own claim to the throne.

21. Monument in the churchyard of St Paul's Cathedral, where public sermons were preached.

22. Political behaviour against the house of York.

23. 27th October.

24. Thomas Bourchier (c.1404–86), Archbishop of Canterbury 1454–86 and Lord Chancellor 1455–6; he crowned both Richard III and Henry VII.

25. Holy Roman Emperor.

26. i.e. the present king, Henry VII.

27. This parenthesis is in the original manuscript but was removed from the printed edition on the order of King James I.

28. i.e. by a certain date.

29. i.e. naturalised foreigners were still to pay the higher rate of customs that was charged to non-naturalised foreigners.

30. Foreign traders – the largest group being Italian – were fined if they did not spend the earnings they made from imports on English goods. The king then took this revenue for himself.

31. A mark was equal to two-thirds of a pound; therefore £4,000.

32. John Morton (c.1420–1500), statesman and cardinal. He was made Archbishop of Canterbury in 1486, Chancellor in 1487 and a cardinal in 1493.

33. Richard Fox or Foxe (c.1448–1528), clergyman.

34. The equivalent to a year's income, paid by those newly appointed to benefices. English kings claimed this for themselves.

35. The north of England, particularly Yorkshire.

36. Francis Viscount Lovel (1457–87), a supporter of Richard III who fought for him at Bosworth; Humphrey Stafford, who had also fought for Richard.

37. i.e. the herald's proclamations of pardon were most effective in putting down the rebellion.

38. Margaret of York (1446–1503), also known as Margaret of Burgundy, sister of Kings Edward IV and Richard III.

39. Lambert Simnel (c.1475–1535), pretender to the throne. He bore some resemblance to Edward IV.

40. Elizabeth Woodville (1437–92), Queen consort of Edward IV, and mother of Elizabeth of York.

41. In support of the king.

42. Henry VII had a palace in Sheen (now Richmond).

43. Elizabeth Woodville was first married to Sir John Grey, 7th Baron Ferrers of Groby, who had fought for the house of Lancaster. On his death she had appealed to Edward IV to have his confiscated estate returned.

44. Declared illegitimate.

45. Queens' College was actually founded in 1448 by Margaret of Anjou. It was refounded by Elizabeth in 1465.

46. i.e. Henry seized her lands and goods.

47. i.e. was ready to give him a sympathetic hearing.

48. i.e. to make their king acceptable to the people.

49. Take note of, acknowledge.

50. St Paul's Cross (see note 21).

51. Pope Innocent VIII (1432–1492), pope from 1484 until his death. His Pontificate was notoriously corrupt.

52. Aeneas' difficult journey from Troy to Italy is recounted in Virgil's *Aeneid*.

53. Having reincorporated.

54. Charles VIII had given Henry refuge in Brittany when he had been exiled, and supported him in his campaign against Richard III.

55. Those nearest to England.

56. Even if it meant going on pilgrimage.

57. Deteriorated.

58. The Duke of Orleans (1462–1515), who became King Louis XII in 1498.

59. Involved, since he was betrothed to Anne, daughter of the Duke of Brittany.

60. 'Partly into the greatness of France and partly into that of Austria': King Louis XI seized Burgundy in 1477, and the Duke of Burgundy's daughter (who died in 1482) had married Maximilian, Holy Roman Emperor and Archduke of Austria in the same year.

61. i.e. Henry.

62. Funds raised by taxation.

63. Was not favoured.

64. Two rooms at Westminster where the king's council met.

65. The Praetor was a Roman magistrate elected to moderate the law.

66. The Censor was another Roman magistrate, elected for the supervision of public morals.

67. i.e. not punishable by death.

68. Unlawful use of force.

69. Those listed in the king's household.

70. i.e. if intention is made equivalent to action for any accusation not punishable by death.

71. i.e. have to wait a year and a day.

72. The clergy were exempt from criminal proceedings before a common law court.

73. i.e. maintaining retinues of armed servants.

74. Greatest influence.

75. i.e. the earl.

76. Denarius, i.e. any small coin.

77. James III of Scotland.

78. In the person of.

79. A fine was a legal device for the transfer of lands and estates. Henry's new law meant that the lawful transfer of property should be final after a five-year period of the possibility of appeal.

80. i.e. and that it may vary from case to case.

81. Ovid's *Metamorphoses* recounts the story of Cadmus sowing the teeth of a dragon, which grew into armed soldiers.

82. i.e. in the wrong direction, towards forfeitures and the revenue they brought in, rather than obedience.

83. i.e. co-operation between the accused and the informer, often in collaboration, so that when a case was 'faintly prosecuted' and failed, the accused was immune from future prosecution for the same offence.

84. i.e. the oath to pardon the rebels.

85. i.e. pretending that religious scruples demand he not go back on his word.

86. 'Stated as a bride, and solemnly bedded': treated with great state, and displayed on the marriage-bed.

87. Character.

88. A religious order of knights, founded during the crusades.

89. Charlemagne (742–814), King of the Franks 771–814.

90. The 'bastard slip' was Ferdinand I, illegitimate son of Alonso V, King of Aragon and Naples; the 'clear and undoubted right' refers to the fact that the Aragonese dynasty had taken Naples in 1422 from the Angevins, who were of French descent, and thus whose claim Charles inherited.

91. Averroes, Latin form of Ibn Rushd (1126–98), Islamic philosopher, whose commentaries on Aristotle's works were hugely influential.

92. The Duke of Orleans, opposed to Charles.

93. Since Edward III, English kings had also claimed to be kings of France.

94. Henry VIII (1491–1547), King of England 1509–47.

95. John II of France, defeated at Poitiers in 1356 and taken to London as a prisoner.

96. Henry VI, crowned King of France in 1431.

97. Outsiders, 'people from across the mountains' (in this case, the Alps).

98. Overcome.

99. John Morton and Richard Fox (see notes 32 and 33).

100. Nobles and gentry.

101. Saved (money), i.e. they must have money, since they were so sparing with it.

102. Pay dishonestly claimed by commanders for soldiers who were dead or no longer in their service.

103. Landlords who looked after the king's land usually had to pay a fine in order to sell ('alienate') it; this measure was now lifted.

104. i.e. standard weights and measures.

105. Having them believe.

106. The patron saint of Spain.

107. Margaret, Duchess of Burgundy.

108. i.e. making the King of France responsible for the payment, rather than Maximilian, was worth as much as the payment itself.

109. Are usually.

110. The Turks exacted a tribute of children from the Christian inhabitants of territories they had conquered, and trained them as soldiers.

111. Few people could dispute.

112. i.e. although the French did not approve of the act.

113. Footprints that have crossed and recrossed.

114. Foot-soldiers, miners.

115. Philip I of Castile (1478–1506), the son of Maximilian I, who became Emperor of Germany in 1493.

116. William Warham (*c*.1450–1532), a lawyer, who was made Archbishop of Canterbury in 1503 and Lord Chancellor the following year.

117. You may be misled by.

118. Invented by the king and therefore untrustworthy.

119. Prevent.

120. A mistake, corrected in later versions; Margaret's property and rights were gained through marriage, and thus matrimonial rather than patrimonial.

121. Henry.

122. Perkin.

123. Sir William Stanley (?–1495), who had fought decisively for Henry at the battles of Bosworth and Tewkesbury.

124. The future Henry VIII.

125. Arrested.

126. 'Give, and it will be given to you. A good measure, pressed down, shaken together and running over, will be poured into your lap.' (Luke 6:38)

127. Stanley.

128. i.e. both churchmen and lawyers.

129. The area around Dublin that was ruled by the English crown.

130. See below, pp. 145–7.

131. Worked in his favour.

132. Serjeants were high-ranking barristers.

133. The papacy maintained that the Kingdom of Naples was under its sovereignty.

134. Crowned: Edward IV, Edward V (monarch for two months but in fact never crowned) and Richard III; murdered: Edmund, Earl of Rutland, George, Earl of Clarence and the two princes in the Tower, Edward V and Richard, Duke of York.

135. 2 Samuel 24:17.

136. Bind itself.

137. A jury could now be punished for giving a false verdict, and its verdict was no longer regarded as final and binding.

138. i.e. the cost of a new trial would exceed the original sum in question.

139. i.e. the next in line to inherit.

140. 'In the form of a pauper' (Latin).

141. James IV (1473–1513), King of Scotland 1488–1513.

142. Three biblical stories of deliverance: an angel shut the mouths of lions to protect Daniel, God's servant (Daniel 6:22); Joash was a prince, rescued from a massacre of the royal family (2 Kings 11:1–3); an angel intervened to prevent Abraham from sacrificing his son, Isaac (Genesis 22:11–12).

143. Know.

144. Philip.

145. 'Great commerce' (Latin).

146. 'Bad commerce' (Latin).

147. A tax paid in lieu of military service.

148. Speaking to the people together and separately.

149. i.e. always ready to go with the crowd.

150. Seeking popularity.

151. A reference to Plutarch's Life of Alexander the Great, where an Indian sage shows the king a leather skin ('bladder') as an image of his kingdom; pressed down in one place, air in the bladder will rise up in another place. The only way to keep the surface even is to press the centre of the bladder.

152. How important it was to him.

153. Is usual.

154. Agreeing conditions for a peace.

155. To intercept them.

156. i.e. about three feet (one metre) long.

157. A wooden frame on which the condemned man was dragged through the streets to the place of execution.

158. i.e. to buy pardons under the Great Seal.

159. Making out that they were done.

160. A ceremonial cap, symbolising the Pope's approval.

161. Warbeck.

162. Scaling the walls.

163. Matthew 20:1–12 tells the parable of the workers in the vineyard, all of whom received the same pay, despite working different hours.

164. Sebastian Cabot (1474–1557), explorer and navigator, the son of John Cabot.

165. See note 19.

166. Clergy could not be executed.

167. Judges appointed to hear ('oyer') and decide ('determiner') the judgement.

168. Prince Henry (later Henry VIII).

169. That between Charles and Mary.

170. Louis XII (1462–1515), King of France 1498–1515.

171. Shortly after his ascension to the throne, Louis XII occupied Milan, claiming it his by descent.

172. Of Rome.

173. Small coins (see note 76).

174. King Henry and King Ferdinand.

175. Hesperus is the evening star; Arcturus is the brightest star in the constellation Boötes.

176. Alfonso X, 'the Astronomer' or 'the Wise' (1221–84), King of Castile and Leon 1252–84.

177. This was because John of Gaunt was for a time king of Castile, due to his marriage to Constance, daughter of Pedro the Cruel.

178. As the marriage between a man and his brother's widow was forbidden by biblical law, dispensation from the Pope was needed for Henry VIII's marriage to Catherine to take place.

179. Mary Tudor (1516–58), Queen of England and Ireland 1553–8, was the daughter of Henry VIII by his first wife, Catherine of Aragon; Elizabeth (1533–1603), Queen of England 1558–1603, was his daughter by his second wife, Anne Boleyn.

180. 'Even, perhaps, given carnal knowledge' (Latin).

181. When the jury found that there was a case to answer.

182. i.e. imprison them, rather than proceed with the trial.

183. Partial resemblance.

184. Summon.

185. Land tenured directly from the crown.

186. Tenants in chief (*in capite*) were bound by certain conditions; one was that if, on their death, they left an underage heir, he became a ward of the king, which involved payment (wardships). This heir and ward, on coming of age, could not then possess his estate before paying a fee to the king (liveries).

187. The first year's profit of an inherited estate.

188. A fee attached to the alienating – transferring – of property.

189. Evicting those living on land belonging to the king, on little evidence.

190. Deprived of the protection of the law as a result of legal proceedings.

191. See p. 44. The keeping of large numbers of retainers was forbidden, on account of it being a threat to public peace and the king's authority.

192. Related (by marriage).

193. See Revelation 6:9–10: 'I saw under the altar the souls of those who had been slain…'

194. i.e. the day they left their house.

195. A groat was a silver coin worth fourpence, thus groats and half-groats were recoined at three times their face value.

196. Incidental revenue.

197. Exclude him (Philip) from.

198. Ferdinando.

199. Death (represented by Pluto, the god of the underworld) was more advantageous to him than wisdom or cunning (as represented by Pallas, an epithet for Athena, goddess of wisdom).

200. Not of the nobility.

201. Ferdinand.

202. Prince Henry was more popular than King Henry, because of the latter's taxation and perceived greed.

203. Philip.

204. Perplexed.

205. If Ferninand would allow him to govern his kingdom, Philip would be ruled by him in everything else.

206. The *intercursus magnus* (see above, p. 111).

207. Thomas Wolsey (c.1475–1530), English cardinal and statesman. Under Henry VIII he became Archbishop of York, a cardinal, and then Lord Chancellor.

208. 'In the future' (Latin).

209. Of fortune, i.e. irregularity.

210. The Savoy hospital and almshouse.

211. 'Mine and yours' (Latin), i.e. property rights.

212. From responsibility for bad actions.

213. Spies and those receiving salaries (pensions) in return for information.

214. To have his spies publicly cursed, in order for them to appear to be his enemies (see p. 88).

215. Three wise men.

acquest: *acquisition*
addulce: *sweeten, soften*
advertise: *inform*
advoultry: *adultery*
Almain: *Germany*
ambassage: *embassy*
animated: *inspired*
appeach: *accuse*
attentate: *assault*
babies: *dolls, toys*
bannerets: *knights*
bark: *ship*
battle: *division*
bewray: *betray*
bottom: *ship*
boutefeu: firebrand
brandle: *upset*
broach: *spit*
brocage: *trickery*
budget: *wallet*
card: *map, chart*
casualties: *incidental revenues*
casting-counter: *pawn*
catching: *hurried*
caul: *net for covering the head*
chievance: *usurious transaction*
churmne: *confused noise*
close: *secret*
cock-boat: *a small ship's boat*
court-fames: *unofficial court
    newsletters*
cognisance: *badge of an employer*
compound: *settle*
confident: *trustworthy*

courage: *anger, pride*
dart: *small spear*
debonaire: *gentle*
difficile: *unmanageable*
dirigies: dirges
disme: *tithe*
distaste: *to dislike*
dry: *unfruitful*
durance: *imprisonment*
espials: *spies*
fatal: *fated, inevitable*
finder: *procurer*
flies: *spies*
*flagrante crimine: while the
    crime is fresh*
greese: *steps*
grist: *lot*
heart: *pride*
hind: *labourer*
idols: *false images; here
    pretenders to the throne*
impropriate: *appropriate*
inchoation: *beginning*
indifferent: *impartial*
infausting: *misfortune*
inn: *gather*
intend: *attend to, look after*
jointure: *dowry*
laics: *laymen*
leese: *disperse*
lieger: *resident*
long-robe: *cleric*
matronal: *womanly*
mattacina: pantomime

may-game: *sport, revelry associated with May Day celebrations*

mean: *intermediary*

minish: *break up (into parts)*

murrey: *mulberry*

mutined: *mutinous, rebellious*

nocent: *harmful*

no not: *not even*

nuncio: *messenger*

obnoxious: *indebted to*

occurrents: *events*

oppignorated: *pawned*

overseen: *deceived*

pieces: *pictures*

perspective: *inspection*

pill: *rob*

plausible: *praiseworthy*

points: *pieces of lace used for handkerchiefs*

postilled: *noted*

privado: *intimate friend, favourite*

privily: *secretly*

privity: *private knowledge*

privy: *secret*

puncto: *detail, observance*

quarrel: *accuse*

quiet: *secure*

quire: *choir*

rampier: *rampart*

reft: *bereft*

resiance: *residence*

rip up: *spread about*

rode: *raid*

runagate: *vagabond*

sad: *grave, sober*

seen: *skilled*

skein: *short dagger*

sort: *adapt*

staddles: *young trees*

stellionate: *counterfeit merchandise, fraudulence*

strait: *close, strict*

submiss: *submissive*

subtile: *cunning*

surcharge: *impute*

tallages: *tolls*

taskes: *taxes*

temporalty: *secular authorities*

tissick: *consumption*

toil: *trap*

trains: *plots*

treat: *negotiate*

understand: *take note of*

ure: *use*

vent: *make known*

wait upon: *carry out*

wit: *intelligence, understanding*

yield: *give*

Francis Bacon was born in London in 1561, the fifth son of Sir Nicholas Bacon, Lord Keeper to Elizabeth I, and his second wife Lady Anne Cooke, a scholar and translator.

Bacon studied at Trinity College, Cambridge, and as it was intended that he serve in public office, he spent three years with the Queen's ambassador to France, Sir Amias Paulet. However, his father died in 1579 before he had settled an estate on his youngest son and thus, denied an inheritance, Bacon returned to England to become a lawyer.

An able lawyer, Bacon became an MP in 1581, but in 1593 he lost favour with the Queen, after opposing her proposal for heavy taxation. However, he remained employed by the crown on a legal basis.

With the accession to the throne of James I in 1603, Bacon finally achieved public office. He quickly rose in rank, becoming Lord Keeper in 1617 and Lord Chancellor in 1618, the same year that he was made Baron Verulam; in 1621, he was made Viscount St Albans.

Bacon fell out of favour again in 1621 when he was faced with charges of bribery: he was fined, imprisoned, and forced to leave court. At this point he dedicated himself to writing (previous works included the treatise *The Advancement of Learning*), producing *The History of the Reign of King Henry VII*, *Essays* and *New Atlantis* in quick succession.

He contracted pneumonia and died in London in 1626, and was buried in St Albans.

SELECTED TITLES FROM HESPERUS PRESS